The Complete Book of
Stock-Bodied
Drag Racing

Produced by LYLE KENYON ENGEL
with the editorial staff of
Auto Racing **magazine**

SCHOLASTIC BOOK SERVICES
NEW YORK • TORONTO • LONDON • AUCKLAND • SYDNEY • TOKYO

A hardcover edition of this book is published by Four Winds Press, a division of Scholastic, and is available through your local bookstore or directly from FOUR WINDS PRESS, 50 West 44 Street, New York, N.Y. 10036

All photographs courtesy of *Auto Racing* magazine

3rd printing . . . . February 1975
Printed in the U.S.A.

The Complete Book of
Stock-Bodied Drag Racing

CONTENTS

Introduction

This book is the most comprehensive account ever written about the full-bodied segment of drag racing — how it was and how it is today. Covering the early experiments, and the development that was faster than the eye could follow, this book tells the story of the almost unbelievable performance by nitro-burning FXers, the sizzling personal feuds in the superfast gas coupe ranks, and gives invaluable technical advice from winning pro racers.

If this book has a single great feature that stands out from the others it is the unusually detailed historical record of drag racing's stock-bodied divisions — factory stock to A/Gas Supercharged. Racing did not draw crowds of 100,000 in 1950, and there were no eight-second elapsed times — with body or without. Yet many of today's superstars were then cutting their teeth on coupes and roadsters, unaware that drag racing would evolve into the sport that attracted more than eleven million paid spectators last year.

The sight of a favorite new Super Stock bombing off the starting line, wheel to wheel with another rainbow-colored factory rocket, thrills contemporary crowds, and a pair of earthshaking gas coupes with older bodies and giant supercharged engines is enough to take traditional fans back a few years in memory of "the good old days." Newcomers to the sport marvel at the mechanical accomplishment, wondering what it would take to put their own cars on the strip — and how to get in on the fun of a bustling car club.

The Complete Book of Stock-Bodied Drag Racing covers the quarter-mile from preparation to pits, from green light to finish line, from novice to veteran, from race to blood-boiling race.

Mike Doherty

Top: Jay Hamilton, a Lakewood, California veteran, has fine-tuned this '58 Pontiac to the computer-like consistency so necessary in the handicap system, and makes 100-mph racing pay. Hamilton, an E/SA recordholder, nailed the 1966 World Championship, and boasts that the engine only needs bearings once a season—making racing the ultimate in trouble-free profit.

Bottom: The ungainly Hudson Hornets make surprisingly good machines for lower stock classes. The twin "H-Power" sixes of 308 inches put out lots of torque, and took Jack Clifford and Jack Thorpe (among others) to national records and impressive handicap wins over newer cars.

1

The Stockers

Drag racing as a sport has flourished in numbers unlike other forms of auto racing primarily because most drag races consist of 300 or more entries rather than the twenty Grand Prix or thirty-three Indy "500" cars. The ranks are largely amateur, with many drivers in cars that see street use during the week. Only a small portion of those in the drag strip pits are full or semiprofessionals.

Three-quarters of the 300, and of the total annual drag strip entry, are stock cars, virtually unchanged from their assembly line status and often doubling as daily transportation.

The "stockers" may not be the most glamorous quarter-milers, nor the fastest, but they provide a means for safe competition against friends and the experience required to drive faster cars. Since the stocks can make unlimited runs without mechanical difficulty, there is continued activity on the strip. Equally important, drag racing is enthusiastically supported by stock car owners in any community.

EARLY RACERS

The production cars that fill today's A/Stock through U/Stock National Hot Rod Association (NHRA) classes, and through the myriad gradations of the American Hot Rod Association's classes, can probably claim kinship to the very first drag race contestants. Though the first organized drag race was held in 1948, proud owners of horseless carriages certainly must have engaged in impromptu side-by-side competition many years earlier. This interest in the performance, power, and speed of one's automobile led to the development of enormous engines for the superluxury cars of the 1920's, making them the fastest money could buy.

New car advancements brought on the Ford V8 engine (1932) and after World War II the '49 Cadillac and Oldsmobile overhead valve V8's resumed the performance spirit. Street racing prevailed among the "hot ones" right up to the introduction of organized races. Most of the pre-1949 engines were modified for street drags — the stock six-cylinder and flathead V8 power output was quite a bit short of the 500 horses of today's 427-cubic-inch monsters. Dual exhaust pipes, dual carburetion, and milled heads were common improvements for "high performance" use. Such nonfactory "souping" would not be legal for modern stock classes, but it was necessary then in order to pull any exhilarating speed at all from the street machines.

The 1939–40 and 1948 Fords and Mercurys preceded the overhead valve power available in 1949 and remained the wheels of many a would-be racer during the next few years, for the stocker ranks have always included everything through the most powerful new cars of each year (until the advent of Super Stock classes in the '60's).

The new Olds 88, with 135 horsepower, became the runaway leader in stock car performance, followed in succession by Olds models until 1955, when Chevrolet, Dodge, Ford, and Pontiac challenged with new V8 power. The thousands of street-racers-turned-legitimate were hardly speedsters by today's standards, however. Quarter-mile speeds of 65–70 mph by the flatheads rose to 80 by '52 Olds winners, then reached 83.33 mph with Arnie Beswick's Stock Eliminator triumph at the first (1954) World Series of Drag Racing.

Another name-to-be was cutting his teeth on these "big numbers" at a national championship in Texas during the same period. A. J. Foyt took his '54 Olds to his first major race win — the stock category trophy.

Tim Woods, owner of the famed Stone-Woods-Cook gas coupes and funny cars to follow, hit 80.63 mph in 1954, earning an official NHRA record at the wheel of a '53 Olds.

Beswick, the Morrison, Illinois farmer who later led the Pontiac Factory Experimental and funny car efforts, also rode to another early victory with Olds. He topped the '55 NHRA Nationals B/S class at 80.00 mph.

Classification figures of this time reveal a significant shortcoming in the stockers as compared to Detroit iron of 1968. Three classes — A/Stock, B/S, and C/S — took in all stock entries during the early 1950's, with weight to horsepower ratios of 19–22, 23–28, and 29–35 lbs./hp. The fastest 3000-pound car therefore could have only 158 horsepower. By comparison, the 1968 Dodge Coronet 426 hemi boasts 425 underrated horsepower and a weight/power ratio of 8 to 1.

DETROIT SEES THE LIGHT

As the Stock Eliminator bracket gradually gained entry into the schedule of races throughout the country, including some championships, factories annually parlayed the growing enthusiasm and publicity with more powerful models, and entry lists multiplied with the formation of new classes. Detroit factories anticipated the stock trend better than NHRA, and in 1956 produced hot new models. But the most powerful of the production cars — the very models which would spur even more interest in high performance, and the forerunners of today's exciting Super Stocks — were viewed with suspicion by rulesmakers. NHRA rules called for any new car with a ratio of less than 15 pounds per advertised horsepower to be automatically moved into the wild gas coupe section against light, race-built early Ford coupes with late model engines. (By 1968 rules, the same 14.90 lbs./hp. cars would fit in L/Stock, twelfth class from the top by power!)

Those 1956's affected and their new classes were: Studebaker Golden Hawk B/G; Chrysler 300B—C/G, along with the DeSoto Adventurer, Dodge D-500, Ford Interceptor, Mercury with 260 engine, Plymouth Fury, and high performance Pontiac; Buick with export kit—D/G, along with any Chevrolet powered by the Corvette engine.

Other classification changes resulted in four stock brackets: "A" through "D" stock classes covering 15.00 through 27.00 and higher weight/power ratios.

Personalities that would grow with the sport were active in stocks then — indicating that at one time almost every drag racer took a turn in the stockers. In 1956 Darrell Zimmerman, now an NHRA Division Director, won NHRA Regional Honors in a '56 Chevy at 78.94 mph; Bernie Partridge, another present NHRA D.D., topped the West Coast Regional C/S class with a 75-mph '52 Olds; and Doug Thorley, the fastest of 1968 Chevrolet funny car drivers at 192 mph, won D/S in his '38 Buick! Another future manufacturer of headers, Jess Tyree, swept the Southern California Championships B/S title with an 85.71-mph Chevy performance.

Chevys were to dominate stock competition for the next few years, and 1956 was a sign of the things to come. New Chevys won nearly every Regional; then Texan R.C. Jasper took one to the NHRA Nationals A/S crown in 16.37/86.87. There was no Stock Eliminator — the A/S class win supposedly produced the quickest stocker.

A class called Super Stock (S/S) was established to accommodate the factories' hottest models for 1957, and the stock field grew to six classes. They were scheduled into still more major events.

All the factories unloaded bombs in short order. Chevy and Pontiac went to fuel injection, Olds to three carburetors, Lincoln to mammoth 430-inch displacement, Mercury to 335 horsepower, and even the Rambler to 275 horsepower. Chevrolet continued at the top, though Ray & Dixon are on record as the first stock racers to hit 100 mph in the quarter. Their '57 Pontiac (317 horsepower) from Bellflower, California's Suburban Pontiac, earned the distinction.

Arnie Beswick rolled on with his warhorse '54 Olds, emerging with the '57 World Series C/S trophy at an improved 16.15/88.06 clip. Arlen Vanke, from Akron, Ohio, entered the stock bracket a short time later for the first of many major wins. His A/S '58 Chevy did 98.90 mph, winning the week-long National Association of Stock Car Auto Racing (NASCAR) Winter Nationals at Flagler Beach, Florida.

The Chevy-Pontiac battle continued through 1959–60 while other makes failed to live up to their advertising copy. What made these two marques so successful on the drag strips? A combination of factors shared by the GM cousins gave them an advantage not even the sharpest Ford or Chrysler product tuner could match. Most important, their true horsepower capability was much closer to the factory advertised rating than that of any other makes (within 10 percent of any specific advertised figure). In addition, Chevrolet's quick-revving, high-winding engines possessed power beyond the starting line if driven correctly — which reduced traction problems. And the rear overhang of the Chevy was long — a natural for weight transfer.

Pontiac's engines gave a little more brute strength, but they had to pull a few hundred extra pounds with it. Pontiac also had a long rear overhang that assisted traction. Both makes benefitted from a wide variety of axle ratios and optional equipment. The four-speed transmission, introduced by Chevrolet in 1958–59, and available on Pontiacs shortly afterwards, is one example of the technical jump they had on the field. Ford did not have a four-speed until 1961, so their cars were at a considerable disadvantage in gearing and shifting.

Harold Ramsey's Wilmington, Delaware, '57 Chevy won the first official Stock Eliminator title at the 1959 NHRA Nationals, turning 14.94/92.30 in the Super Stock class. Shirley Shahan shifted the family '58 Chevy to Stock Eliminator honors at the annual Bakersfield Championship meet.

Pontiacs turned the tables in 1960 when Beswick's new S/S knocked off the seven-day field at the NHRA/NASCAR Winter Nationals in Florida, edging Ramsey's Chevy. Prizes were not yet what one would call bountiful — he won an Inter-State Training Service scholarship, which, as the saying goes, "you can't eat." Jim Wangers hustled the Royal Pontiac entry to the Nationals stock crown before a crowd of hometown Detroit rooters.

At this point Ford introduced a 360 horsepower

model, improved it to 401 horsepower; Chevy came on with the initial 360 horsepower 409 engine for the '61 season; Pontiac unleashed wilder equipment — and the Super Stocks were clearly defined. (Although Super Stock [Top Stock] Eliminator was not inserted into the scheme of things until 1964, the hottest new cars since 1960 were quite apart from any other stockers new or old, and are therefore covered in chapter 2.)

CLASSIFICATION CHANGES

Rules remained almost unchanged for many years, for "stock" has meant truly stock to NHRA, but, with constant fluctuation, classification more than made up for this stability. The Super Stock class (S/S), as an example, officially became at various times Super Super/Stock (SS/S), Optional Super Stock (O/SS), reverted back to plain old S/S for 1963–64, and eventually blossomed into a slate of twelve separate Super Stock classes (SS/A-F) for 1968. Many of the lower classes have also gone up and down on the alphabet scale, and different associations have assigned them such diverse classifications as Formula 6 G/SA, and Ultra Stock Two, thoroughly negating any attempts at conformity or continuity.

Twenty-eight NHRA stock classes had evolved by 1963. This closer breakdown of weight/power factors resulted in much more competitive racing and almost immediately brought to the fore racers that were to stand out in their respective classes to the present day. Individual cars that would be "natural" winners also stood out from the crowd.

Bruce Morgan became 1961 World Points Champion at the NHRA Nationals, capping a year of widespread racing with his trusty B/S '57 Chevy. He received a new Pontiac from the Hurst Corporation, thus becoming the first stocker to win major prizes in other than a new car. Ray Christian won the Nationals A/SA class in a '60 Plymouth, Lennie Kennedy took D/SA with a '61 Buick that preceded many winning Kennedy Buicks.

The pattern was set by 1962 when Kennedy repeated as D/SA winner, improving his Buick from 15.19 to 14.92 elapsed times, and Ted Harbit proved early Studebakers' merits with a K/S 16.90. The 1961 Pontiacs held nearly all the top stock class records at year's end; Californian Dave Kempton had the A/SA mark of 96.70 with his '62 Plymouth; Russ "Big Daddy" Mathews owned the E/SA speed of 91.46 with a '60 Buick. All of these drivers and cars remained in or near the winner's circle for years to come.

In 1963 Keith Berg entered his '50 Olds (that was still winning in 1968), capturing Winternationals M/S honors in 17.37 seconds. Other "ideal cars" of many classes were evident at the Nationals on Labor Day. Ron Broadhead's '60 Pontiac C/S, Bill Abraham's '62 Pontiac A/SA, and Ramon Lowe's '58 Pontiac D/SA were among the veterans that collected. Others included Don Gay's A/S Pontiac and the Hudson of Thorpe and Clifford.

Epitomizing the qualities of enthusiastic racers

with limited investment, Jack Thorpe and Jack
Clifford drove one '54 Hudson all the way to Indianapolis from California, towing another similar
entry. The pair came on to win both K/S and
L/S at the Nationals in a great lesson about deter-
mination — and Hudsons.

Many official national records of the next years
were held by these same figures. Going into 1965,
Clifford's Hudson topped L/S; Berg's Olds had
dipped to 16.65 M/S times; Broadhead remained
atop C/S at 13.25/107.65; Kempton continued
with his Plymouth, now in C/SA; Ramon Lowe's
'62 Pontiac doubled as E/S and F/S record holder; and Mathews' veteran '60 Buick G/SA hit
93.16 mph. Jere Stahl, from York, Pennsylvania,
had started his '55–'57 Chevy campaign, and held
G, H, and I/S national marks.

LOWER CLASSES GIVEN A CHANCE

The lower classes were finally separated from
the hot new models in 1964 and given a Junior
Stock Eliminator bracket. Eliminator racing is the
only competition that earns significant prize money at drag races, and the Stock Eliminator bracket
always consisted of the top qualifiers by elapsed
time, or of class winners racing heads-up. Super
Stock models were the only entries really eligible
for the Stock Eliminator money. So, at long last,
this new bracket provided both recognition and
big money for the Junior Stocks.

Phil Chisholm, of Lansing, Michigan, won the
first NHRA Nationals Junior Stock Eliminator

title, wresting it from a crowd of class winners via a new handicap system. Willey Cossey, Jere Stahl, Doug Kahl, and other favorites fell before Chisholm met teammate Jon Callendar in the final run. Chisholm's I/SA '64 Chevy wagon won by a technicality when Callendar broke one of the new rules that accompanied the handicap system of elimination. He turned an outstanding 15.63 e.t., which was .11 seconds under the existing national record by which handicaps are figured. The rule prohibits any time more than .10 better than the record, so Callendar lost his bid for glory by .01 second.

The handicap system, established to "equalize" all Junior Stock classes, was based on national class records to prevent "sandbagging," or a deceptive early performance — which could receive a more favorable handicap. If a K/S and an M/S class winner were paired, the M/S would be given a head start equal to the difference of the class records. The green starting light of the "Christmas Tree" (introduced in 1963) would come on that much earlier in the M/Stock's lane and the K/S would play catch-up seconds later.

One reaction to this system was new interest in older, slower, more consistent cars on the part of the bracket's veterans who chose to sacrifice the feel of hot performance for the feel of cold cash. It no longer mattered what the car's performance was in comparison to another class of car in eliminations. The question now was, how close to its class record could a car consistently run? The veterans really bore down once the prize money precedent was set. In fact Callendar reached the Nationals Junior Stock final once again the next year from an entry of 500 stocks. He was nearly foiled again, when a mistaken handicap gave William Spanakos' I/S too great a lead, but on a rerun the '59 Chevy hit the jackpot.

In 1966 the action maintained the theme; Willey Cossey topped the Winternationals; Arlen Vanke won the Springnationals over teammate Bill Abraham in a pair of Pontiacs; Dave Kempton won the Nationals in his battle-wise '62 Plymouth C/SA. He hit 13.08/108.17 to bump Pennsylvanian Ernie Musser's '61 Chevy for the money — a big improvement over his 1964 class win times. Notable Nationals class winners included Vanke, Ted Harbit, Abraham, and Doug Kahl.

Junior Stock World Champion of 1966 was Jay Hamilton, a consistent West Coast winner in a '58 Pontiac. Hamilton's F/SA rode over Bill Abraham in 13.65/102.30 to make the Tulsa World Finals limelight.

In 1967 a name change from Junior Stock to Stock Eliminator reflected the increase in stature the stockers enjoyed. Stock Eliminator became the most lucrative category of drag racing, if one balances expenses against possible earnings. Purses at the 1967 NHRA "Big Four" meets alone totalled $20,000 for stockers, some of which cost less than $1000 race-ready (with an average investment of some $2300). The handicap system provides the less expensive lower class stocks with an opportunity to win money equal to that of the stronger new models. To many racers, such an economic balance is much more attractive than the ascending cost/prize ratio of cars like fuel dragsters.

Winners of these important meets were varied, yet similar in breeding. Graham Douglas won the Winternationals with his B/SA 1960 Pontiac station wagon. Springnationals honors went to Jay Hamilton in his venerable '58 Pontiac E/SA. Late-model hopes rose as Ben Wenzel took the $4000 Nationals purse at the wheel of a new B/S Chevy Camaro. George Cureton emerged World Champion from the year-end Tulsa meet, winning $3000 with a G/SA '56 Chevy panel wagon!

Still another of the conquering General Motors stocks from the vintage years, a '57 M/SA sedan driven by John Barkley, opened the 1968 season by sweeping the Winternationals bracket.

Reigning World Champ Cureton wheeled a Chevy sedan delivery model that became extremely popular on the East Coast. The young lab technician from Wilmington, Delaware, chose a 225-horsepower 1956 panel with automatic transmission after considerable study of the bracket. The G/SA was not near the top in power, but was sufficiently competitive in the handicap system. An automatic transmission provided much more consistency than a stick shift version, and consistency was the name of the game under handicap rules. Cureton's times at Tulsa were steady 14.20's, always just under the original 14.30-second record.

The solid lifter, dual four-barrel 265-inch Chevy engine, one of dozens optional for the car, packed enough power to make racing fun and had a reserve in excess of the rated 225 horsepower. Cureton's car ran 272 cubic inches (just under the .060 overbore maximum) with Forgedtrue pistons and Dykes rings. Ignition was dual point Chevy with 38 degrees advance. Carbs were WCFB Carter. Other choices included Champion UJ18Y spark plugs and Stahl exhaust headers.

The car itself was not altered much — it still carried some of the undercoating — but George did make sure it hit the 3296-pound shipping weight within a few notches on the scale. He removed one of the front seats and the heater, then replaced the heavy stock battery with a lightweight counterpart. Enough weight rested on the rear of this model to make other changes in the front/rear weight balance unnecessary.

Chassis modifications were minor but effective. Shock absorber replacements were Cure-Ride 90–10 in front, Gabriel in the rear. Traction bars were 36-inch models welded up by Cureton. Special Stahl 7.10 x 15 front tires reduced rolling resistance and provided a fat profile in the staging lights that gave the driver another fraction of a second in which to get underway without moving out of the electronic beam for a foul start. Series B–140 M & H 9.00 x 15 tires rode on Cragar rear wheels.

Cureton's drive train was made up of a slightly modified Chevy pickup Hydramatic and high-winding 5.38 to 1 rear gears. He shifted with a Hurst competition linkage. This was the World

Champion's combination that produced a record-smashing 13.65/102.44 best.

BUILDING A WINNING STOCKER

Racing stock class cars is truly racing by the rules. Whereas fuel dragsters have comparatively few restrictions, stockers must conform to literally hundreds of rules and regulations. NHRA rules are the most stringent and the most closely enforced. They are adopted by other sanctioning bodies — with the exception of American Hot Rod Association (AHRA) — and are therefore in effect at approximately 70 percent of the nation's strips. To become familiar with all of the finer points of stock class competition a driver must dive right in and race, take in bench racing sessions of the "old hands," and talk it up at every opportunity with the tech men at the strip.

In addition, there are a few basics the driver must observe in order to pass technical inspection and make it to the asphalt. Engines of 1962 and older manufacture are permitted a maximum cylinder overbore of .060 inches; those from 1963 and later years only .030 to a total maximum displacement of 430 inches. Any enlargement in excess moves the car up to gas coupe or other classification.

Although exhaust header outlets are permitted, mufflers must be retained, and tailpipes must extend at least to the rear axle. A protective flywheel shield is required on all A/S and B/S

entries, and on all solid lifter Chevrolet engines
because of their extremely high rpm range. Locked
rear ends, sometimes employed on budget "street
terrors," are not permitted. Magnesium racing
wheels are also forbidden, although other replacements that are stronger or heavier than stock
wheels are acceptable.

Tire violations are the most common cause of
disqualification. The rear rubber must not exceed
seven inches in tread width, and the tires must
have at least two circumferential grooves in the
tread to avoid technically being real slicks. Care-
lessness or outright fraud are often penalized

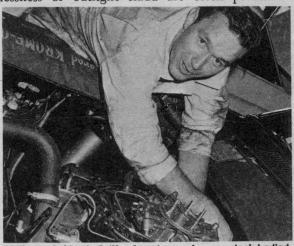

Ed Terry, Oakland, California veteran of many stock-bodied
victories, tunes one of the Ford products he has taken to the
winners circle.

Top: Bill Parnham's E/SA hardtop is seen here in battle with another Southwest stock standout, the 270 horsepower '57 Chevy wagon driven by Jim Hayter. The Ford held its national class record of 107.45 mph into 1968.
Bottom: Sports class racing brings out the stock-looking Corvettes in droves for B through E/SP action. This New Jersey 327 with Jenkins engine is typical of the regular weekend sports racers.

when the tech inspector puts a tape measure on class winners' tires.

Dozens of other considerations — like the fact that traction bars must not exceed one-half the car's wheelbase in length — enter the picture when driving a stocker becomes more than a part-time hobby. But for the multipurpose stock that is driven to the strip, the points mentioned above and those highlighted in the annual rule book will permit safe, economical, yet exciting racing.

Tech inspectors, especially at NHRA strips, give winning cars a thorough going over at race day's end to uncover any violation (even unintentional) of stock class rules. They measure wheelbase and tire width, then check weight. They look for trick mufflers, ballast weight in the trunk and door panels, and other clever gimmicks. They go under the hood to check engine position and visible properties. In case of protest or suspicion they demand that the engine be torn down for certification that camshaft and valve train are legal, head ports are not polished, bore and stroke are stock, the intake manifold is not modified, etc. (They've seen every deception from dummy shock absorbers to lead ballast in the gas tank, so observe stock class rules carefully in order to avoid disqualification.)

Because there are hundreds of stock cars which qualify for the Stock Eliminator bracket, and because those most often chosen by racers are so closely matched, preparing and driving a stocker in serious competition has become a sophisticated science.

Since refinements on a 200-horsepower car are proportionately more crucial — and beneficial — than they are on a 500-horsepower model, the number and degree of modifications and stockers are amazing.

Jere Stahl, holder of innumerable D/S–J/S records and titles during the last five years, and the keenest observer of the stock classes makes the following suggestions, which can be applied to nearly all makes and models. Assuming one has carefully appraised the classes and potential cars, and selected one to race:

BODY. All undercoating and sound deadener should be removed from the underside of the body by heating and scraping. Such weighty excess can also be found on the inside of the car, in door panels, on the floor, and under trunk lid and hood. Study other stock models of the car to make sure of details, then remove radio, heater, column shift, and any other small parts that could have been eliminated by the manufacturer before delivery.

CHASSIS. Carefully inspect all parts, bushings, etc., of the front suspension during preparation as a safety measure and to reduce any unusual friction that might result from the many miles of wear. Replace front shocks with new adjustable Konis or special 20–80 Cure-Rides. Beef up the left front coil spring with at least one wedge to direct the chassis reaction to power. Bolt the ball joints through the A-frames, and remove each rebound snubber to allow more spring travel and front-end lift.

Install adjustable traction bars, preferably the 1964 Ford 427 Fairlane type, and apply spring clips to leaf springs.

ENGINE. The first choice is to have a complete racing setup done by a well-known stock class engine man. However, if a racer is to prepare his own engine, Forgedtrue pistons with .0075- to .009-inch wall clearance are one of the first recommendations. Disassembly of the stock engine goes without saying; use accurate factory specifications in reassembling.

An extra-size oil pan is a worthwhile accessory. It brings the oil level down to below the crankshaft, which increases rpm and power by reducing drag on the crankshaft. An oil breather on each valve cover is also a good idea.

An electric fuel pump, mounted below the level of the gas tank if possible, is essential. Less crucial, but often worth a little extra horsepower, is a fuel line cooler formed from a coil in the line and a "cool can" filled with ice. The mounting is under the hood.

(Naturally his own headers are Stahl's choice, but other name brands are suitable alternates.)

RUNNING GEAR. Slicks or cheater slicks from M & H, Casler, or Goodyear tire companies should be used at 8-28 pounds inflation on most stocks, though the low-pressure models may prove more productive depending on power and whether a standard or automatic transmission is used. Stick shift cars from A through present J or K stock are using M & H wrinkle-walls.

Front wheel width of four inches, with large,

light tires, and rear wheels of six-inch width are standard among the "pros."

Gear ratios and tire circumference, the variables affecting the use of any car's power, can be determined only through trial and error. The majority of cars are using 4.88 through 5.38 cogs, however.

INTERIOR. In cases where there is any lack of clearance, cut out a portion of the front seat for maximum floor shift operation. A remade seat cover will keep it neat and attractive. A heavy duty shifter such as Hurst's, and a Hurst Line/Loc unit — which permits the driver to apply the brakes at the starting line while his feet are occupied on the clutch and gas pedals — are found on nearly all the winning stick shift stockers.

HOTTER STOCKS ARE DIFFERENT

Hot tips for upper class stocks like the 398/400-inch Pontiac GTO's vary somewhat from the winning setup for older cars. With 400 actual horsepower on tap, Pontiac's stock suspension, for instance, has a much better design than older, less powerful cars. "Traction bars" are stock equipment. Air lift bags on the rear coil springs are needed however, to allow "loading" of the chassis for even weight distribution on the rear wheels during acceleration. The right side usually requires more inflation than the left.

Most new cars do not require as extensive a body lightening job as the older numbers, and in Pontiac's case a lightweight version of the GTO which approaches the listed shipping weight of the standard model can be ordered right from the factory. For this car, the driver should purchase the Pontiac part #984716 — a package that adds ten quick horsepower by making the hood scoops functional for fresh air.

Engine work should include an exact "cc'ing" of the combustion chambers, an operation sometimes best left to a quality speed shop. Rules permit the minimum cubic centimeters listed as being within factory tolerances, and the fewer cc the higher the effective compression ratio. A factor of .007-inch of the cylinder head surface per cc can be used to mill the head just enough to attain the highest legal compression ratio.

Thin head gaskets also improve compression, and are legal.

Valve seat grinding of up to ¼-inch into the head is legal and improves the intake flow. Valve springs may be shimmed to reach maximum factory tension specs.

Miscellaneous accessories such as Doug's Headers, an electric fuel pump, Packard 440 ignition wire, Champion J61Y to J66Y plugs, and an intake manifold gasket that blocks off the heat riser passage should replace stock equipment.

Speed tuning maneuvers will involve carburetion, where main jet sizes of the center carb could be enlarged from .062 to .069. Carb jets can go from .068 to .073.

Legal ignition modification, including grinding of the distributor weights, will change the specs from 6 degrees BTC advance with a maximum centrifugal advance of 20–24 crankshaft degrees at 4600 rpm in order to allow the 24 degrees to come in as early as 2400 rpm. This and an initial advance setting of 14 degrees produce a total of 38 degrees advance. A 4-degree camshaft retardation through the use of an offset key is usually helpful in changing the Pontiac's power punch from low rpm to high, where traction is no problem.

New running gear involves wide rear wheels, cheater slicks, and — from the factory — a 2.20 to 1 low gear close-ratio four-speed transmission, 4.33 to 1 rear end with Safe-T-Track differential.

The cost and effort of "building" a stocker today depend on the amount of competition one desires. Slight preparation can total $400 in tires, seat belts, accessories, etc.; more extensive work for serious racing can cost as much as $2500.

The initial investment also depends on one's purpose. A car that will be street driven and raced on weekends may cost more than a model selected specifically for its fit into stock classes. The sharp racers don't let style or age influence a decision on class breaks, shipping weights, etc. Currently, they favor the following cars for winning Stock Eliminator performance: 1954 308-inch Hudsons; 1951–54 Studebaker V8's; 1950 Olds station wagons; 1956–57 Chevy sedan delivery wagons; 1963 Plymouths; and of course a variety of 1956–59 Chevrolet and Pontiac models. There are others, but these cars have proven most profitable. Any buying decision should be preceded by a careful study of the latest classification guide to determine if the car in question compares favorably with any of those mentioned above in its class. Those with shipping weight/advertised horsepower ratios closest to the numerical bottom of any class boundaries are most desirable.

STOCK SPORTS LESS VARIED

Stock sports cars share many characteristics with the stock sedans, though their number is small and their rules slightly more liberal. Corvettes, Porsches, Cobras, early Thunderbirds, and others fill the A/SP through E/SP ranks, qualifying for Street Eliminator competition with class wins. They can use mag racing wheels and any size slicks that will fit on the car. Since they have short wheelbases, performance often exceeds that of stockers with identical engines.

Records in 1968 among the sporty classes included the 10.87/127.11 A/SP marks of Gus Zuidema and his 427 Cobra and the 289 Cobra 11.-71/117.65 C/SP standard of Ed Hedrick. All others were Corvette numbers which ranged from a B/SP 11.35 to an E/SP 12.32. By late 1969 the spread between A/SP and E/SP records had shrunk to a mere three-quarters of a second. Tom Pauser's Corvette was king of the sports classes at 10.79/128.75 while Gene Wilson's Shelby American Mustang was the only non-Corvette record holder with 11.58/117.95 performance.

These statistics are evidence of the close competition and limited scope of stock sports car racing. Very few foreign makes are at all suitable to acceleration, and their owners learned no later than 1956 that the domestic sports models with low gear ratios and big ohv V8 engines were out of reach on the quarter-mile.

The Corvettes have therefore dominated the bracket with only a few exceptions such as Hedrick's consistent Cobra. Hedrick, from Wellsville, New York, represented the sports clan well at the 1967 World Finals, making Street Eliminator round three before his drive line failed embarrassingly on the starting line. Other noteworthy sports competitors over the years include Bruce Larson, who is now in the thick of funny car action, Bruce Morgan, and Earl Wade.

Larson made good use of Cobra potential during 1965–66 by setting the national AA/SP and A/SP records in the Costilow-Larson roadster from Pennsylvania. Initial World Stock Points Champion Morgan turned to a record holding '56 Corvette E/SP for his next season, and was right in contention for the 1962 crown. Wade, now chief mechanic of Don Nicholson's blown fuel funny Comet, topped the A/SP class often in 1960–61, taking Winternationals class honors.

During early years the sports car fraternity faced a certain cynicism from racers in other classes, stemming from the old "teabag set" image created by English imports. Then, as domestic models virtually ousted the "furriners" from contention, the sports entries were overshadowed by the impressive full-size sedans. Today they are content to race and fraternize with each other rather than mix much with racers from other brackets. Theirs is a sport within a sport.

Top: Seen here between the first speed light and the finish line (a 66-foot span), Ronnie Sox and Ron Mancini decide Super Stock Eliminator of 1967 Springnationals by a whisker. Sox, in a faster new hemi, had given Mancini a handicap lead, and then sped to a bumper's win.

Bottom: This attractive Olds, a '68 Cutlass, is a manifestation of the new enthusiasm for the Stock Eliminator category. Towed to Pomona (California) for the Winternationals, the Olds made a trophy run showing for its sponsor.

2

The Super Stocks

The high-performance boom that originated in stock classes during the late 1950's expanded rapidly, and when the factories became more aggressive a Super Stock label was pinned on the hottest new cars. "Supers" actually originated in 1957 with the likes of Chevy's 270-horse bomb and Ford's supercharged answer, but only by 1960 did a distinct separation between S/S and other classes become apparent. New car racing began to command the first respect shown by hot car racers, the sanctioning organizations recognized the Super Stocks for records and eliminator competition, and big gains in horsepower made stock-bodied racing a lot more exciting.

Spectators saw their own cars powering down the nation's strips, and this made Super Stocks a most popular part of every meet. In the pits they talked about how hot the new Fords were, or whether the new Impala could shut off a loaded Dodge. Such consuming interest by local drivers of the same make as those driven by the quarter-mile standouts is the reason for the Super Stock popularity of today. And although the prizes were initially only trophies, the satisfaction of shutting off hot rods and modified cars, and of driving the "hottest thing going" on the street, was more than enough incentive for competition.

In the era of the Super Stocks, Chevrolet and Pontiac held a hammerlock on the other brands. Their power, four-speed transmissions, and co-operative chassis kept them out of reach until 1962, when Dodge and Plymouth emerged to challenge, then take command from 1963 to the present. Ford had brief flashes of success during the decade, but in general the Dearborn entries were too heavy and suffered from exaggerated factory power ratings. Chevy, with 335 horsepower from 348 cubic inches, and Pontiac, with 348 horsepower and 389 inches — both with triple carburetion — were faced in 1960 by Dodge-Plymouth's 330-horsepower 383-cubic-inch dual quad engine and Ford's single four-barrel 360-horse entry.

General Motors' running start at the S/S period paid off, as Jim Wangers won the NHRA Nationals stock honors in his '60 Pontiac. A 14.14/ 102.04 overshadowed Al Eckstrand's 14.51/97.82 in a '60 Plymouth automatic.

Ford developed a three two-barrel carb system, and other racing features for a 401-horsepower rating on its new 390-cubic-inch engine. It was immediately competitive, as proven by Les Ritchey's outstanding 13.33/105.50 clocking at the 1961 Winternationals. But the 390 was not a race design, and it was done under by the mighty new 409 Chevys.

Don Nicholson assumed the Super Stock throne when he tooled his Pasadena '61 Chevy 409 to 13.59/105.88 times at the meet. Frank Sanders, from Phoenix, won the S/S class in another 409, clocking 13.63/105.88. These were the original 409's, rated conservatively at 360 horsepower, that coupled with four-speed transmissions and 4.56 rear end gears were natural winners of their year. Only a handful of highly modified Pontiacs, rated at 363 horsepower from 389 cubic inches, dulled the Chevy sparkle. Hayden Proffitt rang up a strong 12.55/110.29 Optional Super/Stock win at the later Nationals, and Arnie Beswick got S/S in another Pontiac, but the Eliminator title escaped both camps when Nicholson and Beswick, the finalists, were both disqualified on the trophy run!

Year-end OS/S national records were held by Pennsylvanian Dave Strickler's 409 at 13.24 seconds, and Hayden Proffitt's Pontiac at 109.22 mph.

Proffitt's 12.75/111.94 Pontiac times at the '62 Winternationals were impressive, with wicked 6500-rpm shifts, but the Stock Eliminator go matched Nicholson and Strickler 409 Chevys. A superb start by the California star held off Strickler's amazing 12.55 with 12.84/109.22 performance. Ford's 406 and Chrysler's 413 did not show any threatening strength.

DETROIT GOES WILD

The various factory horses for the year included the 409-horse 409, now with dual quads, 420-horse 413 Dodge Darts and Plymouths, Ford's 405-horse 406 dark horse, and a 421-cubic-inch brute from Pontiac.

Detroit firms had gone to incredible lengths in seeking to rule the racing roost. Pontiac, for instance, offered aluminum front end pieces and bumpers, aluminum exhaust headers, adjustable fan, Hurst shift linkage, wide wheels, and enough high-performance options to fill a four-page list.

Race-inspired four-speed transmissions were available on Buick, Chevrolet, Ford, Mercury, Olds, Pontiac, and Studebaker, suddenly popular after being developed initially for the 1956 Corvette.

Dodge matched its new race engine with a chassis on which police car springs and shock absorbers were fitted for resistance to rear wheel hop and spring wrap-up. On the same chassis, the rear pinion snubber was beefed by the factory — a standard "trick" among those racing the stocks. Extra-wide (6½-inch) wheels were available for the rear. The drive line was entirely heavy-duty. The cost of the complete 420-horsepower option? A deficit price of $684 to the company.

A headline match race between the leading drivers of two rival camps typified Super Stock racing in 1962. Don Nicholson and the Detroit Ramchargers Club, a group of Chrysler Corporation engineers, met at Detroit Dragway. The

Chevy boasted a 425-horse "Mark VI" 409 version, weighed 3660 pounds. A four-speed and 4.88 rear combination, with stock Vogue Premium 9.00 x 14 tires, produced a winning 12.74 e.t.

The Rams' 413 Dart, rated at 420 horsepower, weighed only 3400 pounds, but suffered with a balky three-speed transmission. The new M & H Super Stock tires and 4.56 gears led to a close and interesting match with the Chevy.

The big meeting of the year, the NHRA Nationals on Labor Day, drew nearly every top Super in the country for another Chevy score. Hayden Proffitt sailed past the Ramchargers in 12.83/113.92 with his 409, following up his triumph at the Detroit World Championships. Bud Faubel, Al Eckstrand, and Bill "Maverick" Golden were among MoPar threats from across the country.

Even a month earlier Tom Grove had recorded the first 11-second elapsed time by a stock car with his '62 Plymouth SS/S. He clocked 11.93/118.57 at Fremont (California) Dragway. And although Proffitt hit 11.96 later in the year, this signaled the beginning of the end for GM products. Even before GM's 1963 "performance ban," MoPars (so called because Chrysler's parts division has the name) began to march. "Maverick" Golden held both ends of the national SS/SA record with his Dodge during the year, and as 1963 opened Dick Ladeen, from Portland, owned the SS/S e.t. mark of 12.71 with a Dodge, and Dick Harrell's Chevy 111.47 was tops. There were many better times recorded, especially in West Coast racing, but these were often accomplished with cars that would not meet rigid stock rules. Dave Simerly led the California clan with 12 flat e.t.'s in the famed Dave's Chevron SS/S Dodge.

A racer making a name for himself in dragsters was storming the Southeast in a 413 Dodge at the same time. Don Garlits tried his hand with the Super Stocks during 1962–63, hustling a best of 12.40/115 before the 426 made a debut.

"Maverick," from Sun Valley, California, opened the 1963 season by turning steady 12.10's in a streak of five consecutive Stock Eliminator wins at Pomona against the tough Coast competition. The MoPar era was opened. The following Winternationals went to Detroit attorney Al Eckstrand in the Ramchargers' hot new 426 Dodge automatic. A 12.44/115.08 edged the Golden Commandos team (their hometown rivals) and their '63 Plymouth. Tom Grove and Bill Hanyon won top classes in other Plymouths.

Eckstrand won a set of tools and cabinet, a Honda motorcycle, some free oil, and an ignition system for a national victory that had required a cross-country tow, a week-long stay in California, and expensive preparation! The $16,000 Super Stock payoff of 1967 was still far in the future.

One of the many rules that have governed Super Stock racing at one time or another was in effect at this meet: The drivers eligible for Stock Eliminator were prohibited from opening their hoods during continuous racing until a winner emerged. They could not add water, oil, or make minor adjustments between rounds under the provisions of this ruling, which was short-lived.

NHRA LIMITS RADICAL SUPERS

The SS/S designation was changed to S/S for 1963, and limits were placed on displacement and weight. NHRA foresaw a wild factory duel for drag racing supremacy. It established a 427.2-cubic-inch maximum for Super Stocks, and a 7.5 pounds per cubic inch minimum weight (3200 pounds) to prevent the development of really radical factory machines.

In conjunction with the 427 rule, then, came the new engines — 427 Chevy, 427 Ford, 426 Mo-Par — each a race design with power plus. The wild Z-11 Chevy engine of more than 500 horse-power, the 13.5 to 1 compression ratio of Chrysler's 426, and severe weight reduction programs of Ford and Pontiac were evidence that Detroit valued drag strip publicity enough to spend millions on special equipment.

Ford introduced fiberglass body panels and a lightweight frame to cut 700 pounds off the 4150-pound bulk of its Galaxie, the only way it could become competitive with the lighter MoPars. Pontiac went even further with its famed "Swiss Cheese" 1963 models that boasted liberal body aluminum and frames so drilled with lightening holes that they often twisted under acceleration. The Pontiacs were not built in any quantity, however, and they fell into the Factory Experimental class rather than the Super Stock.

The going got so wild that new parts and engine options were made available almost daily. Chrysler released a "Stage II" 426 package before

Plymouth's new Super Commando 426—the hemi—was announced in February, 1964. This brute with 12.5 to 1 compression and dual four-barrels, identical to the Dodge Hemi-Charger 426 in all but name, went on to rule the stock-bodied classes.

Top: Super Stock racing is a big business for Sox and Martin of Burlington, North Carolina. They bring this impressive rig to their Plymouth Super Car Clinics *en route* to races.
Bottom: The popularity of the Super Stocks on the East Coast was never better illustrated than by a busload of avid Bill Flynn fans. They traveled to Connecticut Dragway to see a match race involving his Dodge.

the initial version even had a chance to cool down. Stage II, released in June, offered 17 percent more carburetor venturi area and increased camshaft lift and duration. Chevy's wild Z-11 kit for the 427, a $1250 option, and miscellaneous Ford and Pontiac parts kept racers busier hustling parts between races than they were on the strips.

"NAMES" AND FACTORY TEAMS EMERGE

Factory "arrangements" enabled certain "name" racers to obtain the latest goodies far in advance of their competitors, and while they vigorously deny it to this day, most of the manufacturers had this kind of setup. The results on the strips indicate who did and who did not receive the hot parts that produced another boost in horsepower or reduced weight a few pounds.

NHRA Nationals Stock Eliminator, for instance, paired two familiar names in the final round: the Ramchargers versus their former driver Al Eckstrand. These two cars, both Dodges, both conveniently near the factories in Detroit, are good examples of the factories' influence on Super Stocks as well as on the drivers' ability.

Herman Mozer drove the Rams' candy-striped model to an eyelash win over "Lawman" Eckstrand, 12.22/116.73 to 12.23/114.94. Those in attendance at this "coming out party for Super Stocks" remember the money run as one of the closest big events in drag racing.

A totally unsponsored novice named Dick Dyke

upset the pros with an absolutely stock Plymouth during mid-'63, however, giving hope to the hundreds of other amateur drivers of Supers around the country. Dyke, from Sioux City, Iowa, bought an early aluminum 426, learned about rear spring clips and boosting of automatic transmission line pressure, and went racing. A 12.32 e.t. the first time out was hard to believe, but the Stage I wedge ran 11.95 to 12.20 every time thereafter, although the engine had never been touched.

He won the *Drag News* Invitational and was runner-up to Proffitt at the Detroit World Championships in weeks preceding Labor Day. In both cases he went over Nicholson, the Ramchargers, "Maverick," and all. When he missed the NHRA Nationals entry, he towed all the way to Texas nonstop and won the AHRA Championships! Experts just scratched their heads as the newcomer unbolted the engine in the Detroit postrace tech inspection for the first time since he got the car.

Late in the year, Dick Brannan, a leader of the Dearborn effort, along with Gas Ronda, Les Ritchey, and Bill Lawton, held the Super Stock national record of 12.42 seconds — not as quick as many weekly times, but officially recorded under supervised record conditions.

Chevrolet and Pontiac had either failed to produce the required 100 units of their hot models, or they had otherwise breached Super Stock rules with aluminum bodies. They were classified Factory Experimental, and were therefore not in direct competition with the Supers.

Many of the Super Stocks did double as FX machines by this time, though, as they were caught in the influence of "outlaw" racing down South. Southern Super Stocks were gutted inside. Carpets and dashboards were removed, as were mufflers, tailpipes, and bumpers, and to add spice to the game they burned nitrated gas. Inasmuch as the Southern strips offered generous match race money, many of the well-known Supers were modified for FX going before the factories actually produced legitimate Factory Experimental models.

As the 1964 season got underway the results of Detroit development since evaluation of the '63 performance became apparent. Chrysler unveiled a monster hemispherical combustion chamber 426 which was to keep MoPars on top from that moment on. The hemis were cloaked in aluminum Dodge and Plymouth bodies for Super Stock class, coupled wth an improved TorqueFlite automatic.

Finally convinced that their heavy sedans would not be consistent winners, Ford came up with the wildest car yet to emanate from the factories — the 427-inch fiberglass Fairlane. Ford was careful to comply with the 1964 rules, and the new threat qualified for S/S.

The Thunderbolts were complete with light plexiglass windows, bubble hood with air ducts, and beefy traction bars on a short wheelbase. They weighed only 3225 pounds race-ready with 427 high-riser engine.

Ford was back in the act but, as it was to discover, the hemis were fantastically strong. Many of the major wins during following months went to a well-subsidized MoPar team. Tom Grove sailed home in his colorful "Melrose Missile" Stage III wedge 426 Plymouth at the Winternationals just prior to hemi eligibility. A final round 11.63/124.13 win was over Doug Lovegrove in a nearly identical Plymouth.

Gas Ronda and Butch Leal powered through the Super Stock field of the *Hot Rod* magazine meet in T-bolts, grabbing the honors for an enthusiastic Ford group. But the new MoPars, with aluminum panels, plexiglass windows, trunk-mounted battery, wide wheels of their own, hemi power, and no rear seat, were tough in the hands of the veteran Chrysler drivers and many former GM stars such as Proffitt.

A seven-inch tire width rule, applied to the Super Stocks (though not the FXers), effectively penalized the stick shift cars, specifically the Fords that had no suitable automatic transmission. Drivers could not run their engines up and use the snap clutch release on the line without excessive wheelspin, so the TorqueFlite pilots who could run their engines up against the brakes for quick starts had a decided advantage.

The tire rule was waived at Detroit Dragway's annual Super Stock Championship just prior to the Nationals, though, and the two makes battled to a virtual draw. T-bolts of Len Richter, Ronda, Lawton, and Leal turned up 11.50/122 results with slicks; numerous MoPars hit 11.40/125. After a leaping start by the Fairlanes, the hemis made up ground, often winning in the last 100 feet of the course.

The following weekend was all hemi. Roger Lindamood, a converted circle track driver, hustled through the cream of the crop at Indy with his "Color Me Gone" S/SA Dodge. He won the first separate Top Stock Eliminator crown, solely for Super Stocks, at 11.31/127.84, passing Jim Thornton in the Ramchargers entry 11.31 to 11.47. Thunderbolts ran 11.80's, and only Butch Leal could qualify one for the Eliminator.

"Maverick" was setting top stock speed of 128 mph in the AHRA Championships at the same time, while Phil Bonner netted the Mr. Stock Eliminator title with a T-bolt.

Ronda, a former dance teacher from West Covina, California, made Ford's whole Thunderbolt project worthwhile when he closed the year as World Stock Eliminator Champion and S/S record holder. The crafty pro had diligently campaigned across the country at numerous NHRA points and record meets, reaching a total of 185 points, twice as many as his nearest challenger. His tangible rewards were a vast array of valuable merchandise and, ironically, a new Plymouth Barracuda.

More rules changes affected 1965 racing. NHRA made speed equipment camshafts legal in S/S and FX classes for the first time, and simultaneously raised the weight-to-displacement minimum from 7.5–1 to 8.0–1 to compensate for the increase in power. The cam rule came about because the problem of inspection and disqualification of the many Super Stock cams became an almost impossible burden on tech committees. It was easier to throw the door open than to enforce the traditional stock rules.

HANDICAP SYSTEM CHANGES THE PICTURE

Most significant of all new methods was the adoption of a handicap system of eliminations for the Springnationals. This race plan was intended to enable those drivers with other than the hottest class of cars to compete with the Super Stocks by providing them with a "head start" equal to the time difference between their respective national class records. This system knocked out some of the incentive to own and race the top-powered Super Stocks because slower, more consistent cars were more likely to win with a handicap. Factories no longer had reason to build ever-wilder equipment for the S/S division, so they maintained their level in the bracket and went to funny cars for real racing performance.

The news did not come out, however, until Ford had created 427-inch Mustangs in a further effort to get Chrysler's scalp. They fit into the Winternationals FX class, unfortunately, and the Top Stock battle was left exclusively to MoPar. Bill Jenkins, recently moved over from his Chevy alignment, was the heads-up bracket winner in 11.39/126.05 with a '65 hemi Plymouth.

Many of the big names of stock-bodied racing had moved into the Factory Experimental arena by this time, including most of the Super Stock heroes through 1964. It was obvious that crowds were more excited by the ten-second FXs than the slower Supers, and promoters would pay more for their appearance. Besides, it was more fun to drive the radical new FX chargers.

Chrysler FX models caused a commotion with altered wheelbases that resulted in the term "funny car." Countering Ford's move of stuffing a 427 engine into a compact, Chrysler engineers moved the rear wheels forward some fifteen inches and the front wheels ten inches on standard size sedans, resulting in a tremendous weight shift.

The Sox & Martin 10.76 e.t. and Ramchargers 132.15 mph speed of the year's first meet proved the value of such bodywork, and opened up the whole era of FX-funny car racing.

So it went through the year, as NHRA Super Stock Eliminator titles fell via handicap to '64 Ford 427 Galaxie AA/SA's of Mike Schmitt and others. MoPars bagged the AHRA Winter Nationals (Ramchargers), Detroit World Championships (Bill Shirey), Cordova World Series (Lee Smith), and NHRA World Points Championship (Joe Smith).

Plymouths were so numerous during 1966 that they came away with every big win, including the first championship title won by a female driver. Shirley Shahan, from Tulare, California, led off the 426 year by embarrassing dozens of name Supers with her '65 Plymouth. She became Top Stock Eliminator of the Winternationals in 11.26/126.76. Butch Leal, in a Plymouth at the time, topped the following *Hot Rod* meet in 11.65/124.30, and Jere Stahl took over to sweep the

Springnationals, Nationals, and the World Championship with his four-speed A/S street hemi.

Stahl dueled continuously with hometown archrival Bill Jenkins who returned to Chevrolet, fielding a 327 Chevy II. The Nationals Eliminator final went 11.73 to 11.76 for the MoPar. A reenactment in the money run of the World Finals found Stahl at 11.65, Jenkins again oh-so-close at 11.73!

Chrysler timed this success with the introduction of a new promotion known as Performance Clinics. Dick Landy, with a Dodge, and Ronnie Sox and his Plymouth were selected to hold high-performance sessions in dealer showrooms for the public in every major city, following up each clinic with an appearance at the local drag strip. These clinics proved so popular that they were expanded to include several Landy and Sox & Martin cars.

Their efforts did a great deal to advance the Super Stock image in the minds of racers and the general public. These "teams" made the major national meets for consistent wins, but did not otherwise compete with weekend drivers. Both programs were enlarged for 1967–68 to also include less elaborate clinics held on a local level by numerous drivers of Dodge-Plymouth products, and they continued to spread the good word about stock-bodied high-performance.

ENTHUSIASTIC S/S COMEBACK

Astute racers observing the S/S scene knew 1967 would be something of a "comeback period." Detroit had made informal announcements that it would be more interested in Super Stock Eliminator this year, reducing its emphasis on the funny car.

Equally important, a complete slate of Super Stock classes was established to accommodate more makes and models. Cars of 1962 and later manufacture became eligible to race the newer ones if their weight-to-power ratio was sufficient. Ten classes, designated SS/A-E and SS/AA-EA ranged from 0.00–6.99 pounds per advertised horsepower to 9.50 and up. Suddenly the Super Stock fraternity was no longer a new car clique, but a varied bracket with many additional entries.

This brought on all sorts of serious attempts at the Super Stock gold, the most effective of which were by Plymouth and a handful of Camaros. Ronnie Sox took an SS/B '67 Plymouth past Ron Mancini's '63 in a Springnationals Plymouth final. The meet gave quite graphic evidence of the sandbagging by S/S cars under the handicap system. Top-quality entries were capable of exceeding their class records by more than the allowed .10 second at the big meets. As a result, the racing became more a question of how close one could come to the record rather than how one accelerated from start to finish. Brake lights came on far too often as contenders approached the finish line thinking that perhaps they had gone too fast.

The most capable of the "manipulators" was Bill Jenkins in his SS/C 396 Camaro. The Chevy wizard was never near full potential of his mount, even while winning the Nationals with 11.55/ 115.97 times. His strong four-speed entry had turned 11.00/123 on many previous occasions.

Mancini was disqualified in the semifinals for running too quickly, or he would have been Jenkins' last opponent. It was Bob Brown in a '65 Plymouth SS/A who attempted to catch the calculating Camaro handler for $5000. Jenkins was a pronounced crowd favorite in the Chevy, and he got a standing ovation from the 35,000 spectators for beating the "factory teams" with a make that was not officially in racing.

A huge turnout of famous drivers made up the SS/B class in the hottest '67 models. Ronnie Sox, Don Nicholson, Hubert Platt, Dick Landy, Arlen Vanke, and Ed Schartman met heads-up in "B." Ford threw new lightweight two-door sedans and 427 engines with exotic tunnel port heads and manifolds against the 426 MoPars, actually winning the class, but Ed Terry's '67-equipped 1966 model was declared illegal.

The determined preparation for major meets by manufacturers is part of the excitement, the lure, of Super Stock racing today. Cloak-and-dagger activity by Detroit factory departments called "Special Vehicles," "Performance Activities," or "Product Planning" involves "borrowing" of the competition's specifications from unnamed sources, lobbying with rulesmaking organizations like NHRA and AHRA for best treatment in classification of new equipment, and careful study of all the opponents before and during the races.

Top: Gas Ronda appeared in one of the few Cobra Jet Fords that was ready in time for the '68 Winternationals. These 3200-pound Super Stock contenders proved so strong in the hands of Hubert Platt, Ronda, and Super Stock Eliminator Al Joniec that they could dive under the SS/E record at will. The 428-inch engine conservatively rated at 335 horsepower put Ford in the race once again.

Bottom: Stock-bodied cars can use only pump gasoline for fuel, and they are regularly checked at major meets. Tests for nitro additives and even for the blending of two or more brands of gas, are made from samples taken right from the car. The racer is disqualified if the results indicate any "hyping."

Top: Hank Taylor, 16-year-old speedster from Texas, graduated to an aluminum hemi Plymouth for 1964, and set numerous strip and national records. Prepared by Hayden Proffitt, this was one of the very light Chrysler efforts without a back seat, using drilled front seat mounting, single exhaust, etc.
Bottom: Thunderbolt success reached a peak when Butch Leal and Gas Ronda met for *Hot Rod* magazine Super Stock Eliminator honors. The first factory installation of big engines in compact bodies were these fiberglass Fairlanes, but despite their advantages, MoPar hemi won most of the big ones. Pinned hoods, bubble with air scoop, air ducts from headlight openings in grille, fiberglass bumpers, and mag wheels caused a sensation in stock ranks.

It was one of these factory "special forces" that detected Ed Terry's combination of 1966–67 parts and pointed it out to the tech officials.

Factories have on occasion gone so far as to send out "marginally legal" cars capable of sub-record times in order to knock off leading contenders in Eliminator action, thus making room for a perfectly legal teammate to win as the former drops out on a deliberate red light loss. Such is the degree of enthusiasm in today's Super Stock ranks.

Ed Miller, an unsponsored class winner at many important races of the past several years, made drag racing history in winning the year-end 1967 World Super Stock Champion title — and $16,-000. This purse, the largest ever earned at a single drag race to date in any kind of car, was largely due to the generosity of George Hurst, who donated $10,000 to the Super Stock bracket in the name of Hurst Products.

Miller's Rochester, New York, 1965 Plymouth hemi SS/A took a tension-packed final race from Dick Arons' swift Camaro, but was pushed only to 11.19/114.35 to catch Arons. The MoPar has often run in the ten-second range at 125 mph, so the finish line juggling in catching Arons — but not by too much — once again came into play.

Nevertheless, 1967 was definitely a revival period for Super Stocks, largely because cars were manufactured to fit the classes; automotive firms provided increased contingency prize support; and because of the increased publicity provided by publications and governing associations.

PREPARATION: A SPECIALTY

The art of preparing a top-flight Super Stock for winning performance has developed considerably since the days of the tire change and loosened generator belt. Even as late as 1961 most Super Stocks around the country were driven to the strips on soft butyl rear tires that were actually only passenger car tires, although other than the expensive Vogue Premiums or Casler recaps they were the best traction one could buy. Butyls were not much on street mileage, but they did work slightly better than standard tires at the drags. Removal of hub caps and exhaust header plugs, and sometimes a little ignition adjustment was about all the preparation the average entry received prior to a day of racing. Stock was truly stock.

The "pros," such as Proffitt, Nicholson, Beswick, Ronda, and Strickler had the time, knowledge, and sponsorship necessary to actually set up their machines for winning performance, and their efforts paid off in .2- or .3-second e.t. advantages over novices. Many of their principles are not accepted today, however, because production chassis have improved, power has increased, and tires are immeasurably better.

Proffitt's '61–'62 Chevy 409's, for example, were fitted with stiff station wagon springs up front to elevate the front end, and the weakest springs he could find to lower the rear end when accelerating. Rules permitted a maximum difference from the stock body height of 2½ inches front and back, so the pros raised the front and lowered the rear, figuring this would aid weight transfer. Weak shock absorbers permitted easier body travel when the clutch was released. Proffitt added control arms to the chassis, installed a Hays clutch, wide rear wheels, and 9.00 x 14 Casler cheater slicks.

Engine work included a teardown and specification blueprinting, carburetor and ignition modification within the rules, S & S Headers, and the addition of a Fan-O-Matic fan which released at speed. The novice driver/owner had no real knowledge of the trick refinements in this area such as carb jetting and loose racing engine specs even when he did have the time and money to get totally involved in the problem.

The Chevy body had been cleaned of deadener, and naturally had no radio or heater, which in itself was a mark of a true race car, because most Supers were used for daily transportation and did have all the comfort features. Proffitt's Bel Air two-door weighed 3650 pounds.

THE LATEST METHODS

An example of the most complete and professional setup of 1968 was the job done on Dick Landy's famous SS/B 426 Dodge Charger. His chassis work was not so much different from the earlier cars, except that he did not aim for the up-down weight movement. Actually this was less critical because the abundance of new power required less coaxing to get to the ground.

Front shock absorbers were "broken in" for ease

of travel, but were not absolutely weak like those in the former Chevys. A flexible six-cylinder front torsion bar replaced the heavy-duty version. The rear pinion snubber was shimmed up tight to the floor.

Wheels were 4 x 15 front, 6 x 15 rear, with 7.75 x 15 front rubber and wide 10.50 x 15 Goodyear slicks on the rear, spreading out over the six-inch rim as is the current practice.

Drive line details included a heavy-duty four-speed transmission with "slick shift" modification that permitted much better shifting than had been possible a few years earlier. Landy used a Hurst Competition Plus shifter with Line/Loc activator for the front brakes. The latter held his car firmly on the starting line while his feet were well positioned on clutch and accelerator, an option the Super Stocks of previous years could well have used. The clutch was stock with a Schiefer flywheel protected by an R-C bellhousing. A Dodge Sure-Grip differential carried 4.88 gears.

Landy takes great pains with his racing engines, and as a result almost always has more power than his competition. The 426 had been bored out .005-inch for clearancing, had stock pistons, Dykes rings, .008-inch wall clearance. The crankshaft was stock, with .012-inch con rod clearance, Clevite bearings.

An Iskenderian 590 cam with wild .590-inch lift was installed under the NHRA rule permitting cam replacement, along with an Isky valve spring kit. The installation of this radical cam required a cut in the exhaust valve face.

Carburetion and air flow were improved by smoothing out the intake manifold passages and grinding down its divider. Rejetted dual Carter AFB's were preceded by two Bendix electric fuel pumps, a "cool can," and a filter in the fuel system.

Even the oil system came in for modification. Landy rebuilt the 426 oil pan to lower the oil level beneath the crankshaft, reducing drag. Frame K-member notching and installation of a Milodon oil pickup were part of the job.

Ignition was a hemi distributor with Prestolite transistor using 36 degrees total advance at 1000 rpm. A Motorola Tel-Tale tachometer and Synchro-Start overspeed governor — which limits engine rpm to 8000 in case of a missed shift — were accessories.

Body refinements were few for NHRA SS/B competition at 3650 pounds, but a move to run in AHRA's more liberal rules called for removal of window mechanisms, and other lightening measures, use of aluminum manifold, 13.5 to 1 pistons, etc. The rules variation lowered Landy's e.t.'s from 10.90 to 10.50 seconds.

Chevrolet preparation is best observed on Bill Jenkins' astounding SS/C Camaro. The Pennsylvania veteran, a champion in Chevys for years, set up the new 396-cubic-inch Camaro in such a way that it posted a national record in the mid-11-second range and was closely under it in NHRA racing. But where the rules were not record-based, he let loose for 11.00/123 times. Then, when NHRA "factored" his car as having more poten-

tial than the factory power rating (375 horsepower) indicated, and put him in with the mammoth hemis for 1968, Jenkins came up with
10.90/127 results from the same car!

"Grumpy," as he is known, is the most meticu-
lous of racers. The extent of his attention to the
Camaro is not likely to be equaled by anyone.
His choice of suspension was the opposite of the
"hollow shock absorber" theory, utilizing stiff
front units to prevent the very bobbing many
others have felt was essential for weight transfer.
The stock right rear traction bar was retained, and
Jenkins' own Lakewood bars were added for support. Springs were clamped — the entire suspension is stiff, not wishy-washy.

Jenkins makes tireless adjustments such as alternating between a light and a heavy flywheel
depending on the strip conditions. He uses at
least a half-dozen tire sizes and types to vary his
final effective gear ratio and traction. Camshafts
vary from stock to custom ground.

Among those extraordinary measures that put
his Chevy in a position to influence rules were:
virtual rebuilding of the Holley carburetor and
manifold; replacement of stock ignition wiring
with Packard 535 (selected from many possibilities); plugging of the heat riser passage with fur-
nace cement rather than a gasket; measuring and
weighing Mr. Gasket roller tip rocker arms; the
use of six-cylinder GMC piston pins and a special
tappet valley cover to reduce oil flooding; extensive transmission modifications, and on and on.

Ed Miller, a bricklayer, is not a full-time professional racer like Landy and Jenkins, yet he came away with the World Championship. His '65 Plymouth certainly deserves a technical inspection for any hot tips.

Miller and Kip Guenther fielded the racing hemi with a light front end, bucket seat interior, and aluminum transmission assembly on a budget, although the car was at the top of all Super Stock classes — in SS/A. Unsponsored, Miller restricted nonstock engine parts to an Isky 590 cam and kit, Stahl headers, and Mallory ignition! He used no special pistons, or manifold.

Cure-Ride shocks and traction bars were added to the suspension (though one of the bars was broken during his Tulsa win). Tires were big Stahl replacements on the front, and M & H slicks behind.

When the car went into the grueling World Finals it had a welded crankshaft and a welded block (!) because there was no money for new replacements. It had no shifter, and Miller had to requisition one from Hurst when he arrived at the strip. It was a tired car after two years of steady racing on the East Coast — a car nearly Pure Stock that could still run subrecord times.

It is clear that the basis for Super Stock wins can vary tremendously. The approach is less important than the sound mechanical understanding on which it must be based.

The 1968 NHRA rules prohibited the raising or lowering of the Super Stock bodies, but did permit use of any intake manifold of the same basic configuration as the original stock version, and any size rear tire/wheel combination that would fit into the stock wheel well, i.e., slicks. Trunk-mounted batteries were legal, as were factory-installed fresh air hood scoops, and any flat tappet camshaft. Explosion-proof clutch and flywheel were required, along with seat belts and driver safety helmets.

There were twelve SS classes, SS/A through SS/F and their automatic transmission counterparts, which made room for many cars that were not literally Super Stocks. This system included a

The surprise of the 1968 Winternationals Super Stock action was the upset of Bill Jenkins in the first round. Ed Terry, driving Hubert Platt's tunnel-port lightweight Fairlane, got the jump on the '67 National S/S champ, and held the lead despite low 11-second elapsed time.

variety of makes (such as American Motors) in the Super Stock Eliminator class which would not be there otherwise.

NEW ENTRIES THREATEN

As a matter of fact, the renewed interest in Super Stock racing has prompted even Buick, Oldsmobile, and Pontiac to add many high-performance options to their lines while maintaining their self-imposed 10 to 1 weight-to-power minimum. American Motors, unalterably opposed to any high-performance, much less racing, in previous years, has also joined the fray, giving way to the influence of performance-oriented youth.

Wild cams, ram-air ducting, light bodies, gear ratios up to 5.12 to 1, and racing "how-to" booklets prove these firms' interest. The 400-inch, 360-horsepower GM engines in small bodies make the lower SS classes, with the 390-inch AMC Javelin.

The 1968 Eliminator racing was handicap, and the competition was glad of its .10-second breakout rule because Ford's latest bear, the Cobra Jet Mustang, was so strong that it would have otherwise swept the board. Al Joniec, from Philadelphia, won the Pomona Winternationals Super Stock title in an SS/E Cobra Jet, and at the next big meeting, the *Hot Rod* Magazine Championships, Mustangs driven by Hubert Platt, Ed Terry, and others went as much as .20 beneath their national class e.t. records and were disqualified — even though the drivers coasted across the finish line to avoid such hot times!

The package power was a new 428-cubic-inch (430 was the new limit) wedge head engine rated at 335 horsepower. This was the most realistic factory rating by Ford in many years, making the car a tough competitor. In addition, the lightweight 'Stang, which could be ordered without insulation and deadener, weighed only 3225 pounds.

Platt readied his with stiffer shocks on the rear, Logghe Brothers traction bars, fat front tires, and 10.50 x 15 slicks on seven-inch wheels. The battery rested in the trunk over the right rear tire. Engine preparation included the installation of a deep oil pan and the "Daytona" Ford cam and coordinating Crane valve gear, as well as modification of the distributor for 38 degrees advance at 2500 rpm. The 428 boasted 11.5 to 1 compression and high-rise manifold with connecting fresh air ducts for the Holley carburetor.

The transmission was brought to "slick shift" capability with synchronizer ring work. Rear gearing was 4.71, compatible with a 6300-rpm engine limit. Safety precautions included a Schiefer clutch, a thirty-pound roll cage, a strap loop around the driveshaft, and all required belts and harnesses.

It is almost certain that new powerhouses like this will continue the build-up of the Super Stock bracket in the overall drag racing scene, until someday even the $16,000 Miller win is overshadowed.

For 1969 the number of Super Stock classes was increased to twenty, with most rules remaining essentially the same.

Top: Among the first successful six-cylinder efforts in FX was Ron Root's C/FX 1963 Dart. The slant six, with Offenhauser modifications including four-barrel carburetor, wailed to 7000 rpm, and with a four-speed gearbox hit 13s at 100 mph for Winternationals Eliminator victory.

Bottom: One of the wildest FX machines in theory—not in performance—the Cotton Owens "Cotton Picker" was a '65 Dart with rear mounted 426 hemi engine. Driven during its brief campaign by David Pearson, the extreme FX ran mid-10s.

3

Factory Experimentals

Love for those new cars with 427-cubic-inch engines and wild paint jobs — the same emotion that puts funny cars at the top of present spectator attractions — brought on Factory Experimental racing as early as 1962 when the Super Stocks began to grow wings.

The physical differences between the two designations were few — FX had earmarks like slicks, optional factory goodies, etc. — but it was the picture of the wildest stock-bodied Chevy tangling with the wildest stock-bodied Ford that was the mystique of FX. It grew to be a matter of separating the men from the boys.

Many tricks employed by Super Stock drivers in 1962 were sufficient to cause reclassification to Factory Experimental, especially the practice of gutting the interior and building giant engines so popular in the South, but the first legitimate Factory Experimental hybrid label can be applied to a wild Pontiac Tempest. Mickey Thompson Enterprises, with builder-driver Hayden Proffitt, stuffed a 421 engine (bored out to 434 cubic inches) in the compact early in '62 for A/FX work. The package weighed only 3150 pounds, permitting early 12.20/117 times — and class wins at both the Winternationals and Nationals.

Radical stocks were considered to be those with the nose-up attitude, lightweight front ends, wide wheels, gaudy paint, and lettering — no one had thought to build a hybrid stocker, although the engine swap premise was the very basis of gas coupes. The Tempest, with the advantages of short wheelbase and light total weight, was a pioneer of sorts when it first appeared.

Engine installation was not difficult, but the new power necessitated extensive reworking of the rear end. A big Catalina rear end assembly, complete with suspension, replaced the weaker stock version, and was narrowed nearly six inches to fit without violating NHRA rules prohibiting body cutting around the fender wells.

Proffitt preferred the heavy-duty, three-speed floor shift transmission he successfully used in the big cars; he mated it with Pontiac's heavy-duty clutch and flywheel option.

Later in the season, Lloyd Cox took over the car for Thompson, and by adding the latest engine pieces, including 13.0 to 1 pistons, and replacing the stick shift with a three-speed Hydramatic, he improved results to 11.90/120.

A rival firm had components on the market very similar to the Tempest's, and took up the torch with an FX of its own. The Dragmaster team of Jim Nelson-Dode Martin-Sid Parkinson gave birth to the "Golden Lancer" in their Carlsbad, California, shop after seeing the Tempest's potential at the Winternationals. They jammed a hot 413-inch Dodge engine in the new compact Lancer.

Replacement of the stock six-cylinder engine was done professionally, and included installation of a big Dodge drive line, TorqueFlite transmission, and Traction Masters à la Tempest. But, slicks and all, the Lancer could cut no better than 12.26/115 initial times as an A/FX. Impressive, though hardly sensational when compared to Tom Grove's '63 Winternationals 12.37/114.94 in a legitimate Super Stock.

Aluminum Chevys and Pontiacs in the hands of Ronnie Sox, Hayden Proffitt, Don Nicholson, Bill Shrewsberry, Arnie Beswick, Arlen Vanke, Dave Strickler, and Butch Leal headed the more successful "conventional" cars in NHRA's new Factory Experimental class. Their advantages over their legal S/S brothers were the aluminum front end panels, prototype engine parts, mag wheels, and slicks, resulting in eleven-second elapsed times before 1963 was out.

1963 EXPERIMENTALS 'WAY OUT

Chevrolet's Z-11 version, which sometimes made S/S class in varying rules, was the firm's last serious racing effort — and a good one. Aluminum bumpers and fenders reduced bulk to 3350 pounds, all powered by the new 427-inch, 430-horsepower Chevy dual four-barrel muscle.

Pontiac went not a step, but a mile further with two A/FX models. The famed "Swiss Cheese" aluminum Catalinas gave evidence of factory attention that was hard to believe.

Hood, fenders, splash pan, inner and outer fender panels, radiator bulkhead, front and rear bumpers and brackets were of thin-gauge aluminum that dented with little more than the pressure of a finger. Aluminum was also used for the bellhousing, transmission and differential cases, and exhaust headers.

Front brake drums were thin and light, and exhaust parts were held to a single tailpipe and muffler. All body sealer was omitted during production. Most important, the rectangular frame rails had no bottom side, and were drilled with numerous lightening holes — thus the "Swiss Cheese" tag.

Other signs of special attention included mounting of the battery in the trunk over the right rear tire for traction, the use of stiff front and soft rear springs, lightweight 14- x 17-inch rear wheels, an optional 13.0 to 1 engine compression ratio, and plexiglass windows installed by the dealer.

Power was the proven 421, by then at 420 horsepower with high-rise manifold, in a total weight of only 3250 pounds. Despite such custom manufacture, these beauties were priced at only $4000, an amount far lower than factory cost.

Shortly afterward came compact Tempests with 421 engines, which were much like the original Thompson conversion, but with refinements that led to big numbers. Only a handful of these special '63 Tempests rolled out of Pontiac, and most of them went to the stars who already had Catalinas — Beswick, Vanke, Mickey Thompson.

Two models, coupe and station wagon, made use of a special clutch-activated automatic transmission integrated with the differential. This tremendous weight shift to the rear gave them superior traction, but the transmission's size prevented the use of any rear gear ratio greater than 3.90 to 1, resulting in somewhat limited performance. Even those gears, marginal in strength, lasted only 12 to 15 runs before requiring replacement, an all-day job. Beswick's renowned "Mrs. B's Grocery Getter" wagon produced 11.50 e.t.'s at 3450-pound racing weight.

Bill Shrewsberry hustled a Thompson Tempest to Winternationals A/FX honors in 12.04/116.27 while Ford's fiberglass and Chevy's aluminum ran in a new Limited Production class for cars not generally available to the public.

On the East Coast, Beswick swept the Daytona Winternationals; Ronnie Sox, in a Z-11 Chevy from North Carolina, had already mastered the art of using powdered resin on Southern strips for supertraction; and Malcolm Durham flogged a similar Chevy near the nation's capital.

Arlen Vanke held up Ohio hopes, nailing an 11.89/123.11 national A/FX record with his Anderson Pontiac 421 Tempest shortly before the Nationals. No one could touch Dave Strickler's 12.10/120.16 when the big ones met, though, and the York, Pennsylvania, Z-11 pilot went through the A/FX ranks all the way to Little Eliminator.

Top: This FX-funny car rolled over several times.
Middle: Two popular FX stars, Hayden Proffitt with Merc and Dick Landy with Dodge, stir Loins Drag Strip fans to excitement during a match race.
Bottom: Pete Seaton's injected 396 Chevelle. Note lift of wheels as car leaps off starting line.

Top: Dodge Chargers, were striking in their day (1964), but their performance barely exceeded that of unblown A/FX cars.
Middle: Arnie Beswick's blown Pontiac and Don Nicholson's altered wheelbase Comet pull their front wheels in a 1965 match.
Bottom: Shirley Shahan's hemi Plymouth. Mag wheels, slicks, injector stacks, and resin clouds were all part of new match race action.

The Strickler-Jenkins Chevy featured the latest high-rise 427–430 engine, but not the controversial ball joint extensions which had become so popular as front end lifters on the FX Chevys.

Jim Wangers, Super Stock Eliminator at the '62 Nationals, won a close runner-up to Strickler after his B/FX class win in a '63 Pontiac. Beswick, the only farmer with a three-car racing entourage, drove both Tempests and a Catalina to midyear wins at *Drag News* Invitational and Cordova World Series FX Eliminator.

Standing out among B/FX and lower class creations was the strange combination of Dodge D–100 pickup truck and 413-inch Ramcharger engine of Dick Boynton. The Ram Truck, built by Dragmaster for the San Diego disc jockey, was a dreadnought at 3950 pounds. Despite specially fabricated fiberglass front end panels and lead in the tailgate, the truck's weight distribution was nearly 70/30 — and the wind resistance! But surprising 13.00/112 performances kept it a favorite of Southern California fans.

Early Factory Experimental competition was rather limited in scope compared to its subsequent heyday, yet it illustrated the amazing crowd appeal of stock cars gone-one-better.

MERCURY MAKES WAVES

The field changed appearance in 1964 when Mercury took the big engine/compact theme a little further with 427 Comet entries. Don Nicholson, wooed from his Z-11, led the Merc campaign from his new Atlanta base, mowing down all comers first with a one-off station wagon, then with an even quicker coupe. His controversial "Ugly Duckling" wagon was built on a Ford Falcon wheelbase of 109 inches, and weighed in at 3280 pounds. Factory traction bars, scattershield, wide wheels and slicks, fresh air hood bubble, rear mounted battery, and windows without mechanisms left little need for further preparation.

A high-riser 427 engine with Crane cam and kit hit 7000 screaming rpm with a four-speed transmission on "Dyno Don's" path to times as low as 11.12 seconds before spring. The first wild, leaping FX starts were seen when Merc pilots popped the clutch at full throttle, pulling the front wheels into the air while wide slicks provided maximum bite.

Ronnie Sox, another veteran of the Southern "Run What Ya Brung" racing which had fewer restrictions, moved into a Merc and captured the '64 Winternationals FX Eliminator honors. The final heat matched two Comets, with Sox pulling out an 11.47/123.45 to 11.49 thriller from Nicholson.

Chrysler's much-talked-about hemi engine was supposed to debut at the Pomona meet, but it was held back due to initial problems, and there was little opposition to a Merc sweep.

Tom Sturm advanced the Comet cause with shining 128-mph speeds at Bakersfield, and the trend continued through a season of match racing. When the hemis did arrive, however, the Mercs were hard pressed to stay on top.

Roger Lindamood, former Nationals Super Stock Eliminator, established the national A/FX class record with one of the very first hemis out when he touched 11.22/125.17 at a June meeting in Detroit. Only a short time later the Ramchargers, with a not-quite-FX Super Stock hemi Dodge, blasted out a sterling 10.81/129.68 during a big Cecil County, Maryland, race. Nicholson won that meet at 10.75/127.65, finally topping Bud Faubel's 10.99-second hemi challenge. These were "carburetors and gasoline" times at 3200 pounds.

CHARGERS INTRODUCE S/FX

Simultaneously pointing the way toward the future, the Dodge Chargers, a colorful pair of blown FX models, dazzled a San Diego Raceway crowd with smoking 10.90/133.33 debut exhibition passes, complete with parachute stops. The first Super/FX cars, the Chargers, had been built by gas dragster veteran Jim Nelson for Dodge as a touring duo that would steal the Comets' thunder with exhibition races between themselves. Chrysler officials requested and got a special classification of the blown Dodges from NHRA, a class they never imagined would contain any other entries, much less become the popular funny car bracket of today.

Stock 1964 Dodge 330 two-door sedans, with 426 wedge engines, TorqueFlite transmissions, and the optional aluminum front end package were the Chargers' base. The engines were built

Chrysler introduced this exotic injection system for its hemi pilots in early 1965, and Ronnie Sox promptly rang up the first stock-bodied nine-second time. Modified from Hilborn fuel injection, the system permitted the use of nitro fuel, which came shortly thereafter.

Top: Don Nicholson, always a leader of S/S-FX competition, still ran steel wheels, narrow rear rubber, and full accessories as late as 1963 when he drove this Chevy. The car attitude under acceleration was popular at that time.
Bottom: Most of the Ford team received new Mustang FX mounts, but Phil Bonner built up this wild 427 Fairlane and made it a crowd favorite. Wheelie casters on rear were required after the wheelbase change and the addition of enormous slicks on the Atlanta, Georgia machine. The car was campaigned in '64-'65.

Top: The dual use of the AWB MoPars is indicated by class numbers on the side of the Buckeye-Vernon Plymouth. The injected hemi ran NASCAR Ultra Stock, NHRA C/XS, and carried wheelie casters for airborne exhibition appearances.
Bottom: Introduced just in time for the '64 Winternationals, Comet's drag racing entry was the fiberglass coupe with 427 engine. Former Chevy stars were lured into drivers' seats and they swept the meet's A/FX honors. Sox won, over Nicholson, Proffitt, Shrewsberry, and others in new Mercs.

Top: **Among those who moved from Factory Experimental success to funny car money is Bruce Larson. His injected Chevy became a popular FX despite weight; he then went to a radical funny car for 1967.**
Bottom: **Tom Grove switched to A/FX after a Stock Elim victory at the Winternationals, and ran with the 2%-altered wheelbase boys at the '64 Nationals. He cut low elevens, but suffered a transmission failure during a power shift, and Dave Strickler repeated his FX triumph of the previous year. "The Dodge Boys'" lightweight four-speed hemi won in 11.04—more than a full second faster than in 1963!**

up to be typical gas dragster engines of 480 cubic inches with 6-71 blowers for superperformance, requiring a Moon front fuel tank and an electric water pump to complement the radiator.

Fairly standard shock absorber replacement and mag wheel and traction bar installation were the only improvements on a stock chassis. Safety measures such as a roll bar, parachute, and driver flame suit were as much matters of creating an image of extraordinary speed as of necessity.

Weighing a total of 3500 pounds, the Chargers were more show than go, and it didn't take Jack Chrisman (and others) long to figure that a blown FX could do better. Chrisman — still out of the driver's seat since a serious accident the previous year, and itching for action — had both the knowledge of supercharged engines and the vehicle for the job.

He was promoting a factory/dealer sponsored A/FX fiberglass Comet, with Bill Shrewsberry driving, and extended this rivalry with MoPar to S/FX as well. His wild blown Merc, using direct drive, churned up billows of smoke and flashed 150-mph speeds from its first time out at Fremont (California) Drag Strip, overwhelming the Dodges' numbers. Chrisman subsequently followed the Dodges all over the country trying to provoke a head-on match race with the Chargers driven by Jimmy Nix and Jim Johnson, but factory orders prevented any such confrontation.

Chrisman's Comet, while carrying the hastily granted S/FX classification, contributed the second chapter in the evolution of today's funny cars. Blown fuel 427 engine, set back in the chassis a little, with direct drive, straight front axle, gutted interior, were a step ahead of the Dodges.

MoPar came back as the year progressed, however, and Dave Strickler's new four-speed hemi Dodge shut off the NHRA Nationals A/FX class with 11.04 record strength. Fred Cutler, an ingenious Michigan racer, dominated B/FX with the same hemi power in a Dodge station wagon, going 11.81/121. The Ramchargers, Proffitt, Grove, Lindamood, "Maverick," and other hemi pilots made minor modifications on their stockers and joined the FX war with Nicholson, Ronda, Leal, Sox, and the rest of the Ford-Merc squad. These were the leading match racers through the season.

THE BIG YEAR OF FUNNY CARS

The Year of Factory Experimentals was definitely 1965. It was not only the year of the most competition in the bracket, but of the historic development and release of true funny cars, the next step up the stock-bodied ladder.

The big developments began in late 1964 when Chrysler, parrying Ford's insertion of big 427 engines in compact Fairlane bodies for dual S/S-FX use, designed the original altered wheelbase cars — standard size Dodge and Plymouth sedans — that were given the name "funny cars" by writers present at their debut. Introduced at the AHRA Winternationals, the factory altereds were a sensation, capturing Mr. Stock Eliminator and Top Stock Eliminator titles respectively for Bud Faubel (10.92/128.12) and the Ramchargers (10.90/132.15). Low elapsed time of the group was Sox' 10.76.

Chrysler engineers moved the rear wheels of the AWB's forward 15 inches, and the front wheels up 10 inches, shortening the wheelbase to 111 inches, and providing a terrific 45/55 front/rear weight ratio without ballast. This maneuver was a little premature for NHRA rules, however, so they were limited to AHRA and independent strips.

Ford Motor Company timed the construction of ohc (overhead cam) Mustangs perfectly to fit both sanctioning bodies, but it was so rankled by Chrysler's departure from stock car tradition in altering wheelbases, that Ford brass forbade team drivers to race against the altered MoPars.

Winter meets were divided, then, AHRA to MoPar, NHRA to FoMoCo without opposition. Bill Lawton won the NHRA Factory Stock Eliminator laurels with 10.93/128.70 Mustang times. Nicholson hit 10.90/130.05 in his new ohc Comet. The shocker came in March when Dick Landy, with a few months' time to improve the breed, scorched Bakersfield's quarter in 10.26/138.20. This prompted the Ford move — it was apparent that not even the 427 compacts could match the new MoPars. Ronnie Sox reemphasized this only a month later when he became the first driver of an unblown stock-bodied car to break into the nine-second bracket. His altered Plymouth, fitted with Chrysler's new Hilborn fuel injection system, hit 9.98/136 on April 25, 1965 at York, Pennsylvania.

Landy's Dodge was almost beyond 1965 imagination when it was unleashed at Bakersfield. It weighed a "heavy" 3000 pounds, yet outperformed all but the fastest hot cars at the meet. Fiberglass fenders, hood, doors, dashboard, and bumpers accomplished the same weight savings as the formerly used aluminum, and plexiglass filled the windows all around. Magnesium intake manifold, aluminum cylinder heads and water pump were also employed to bring the big car down to a ton and a half. The California star just beefed the rear pinion snubber right up to the crossmember so that the rear of the car was, in effect, solid, mounted a pair of the new "wrinkle wall" 9.00 x 15 Goodyear slicks, and let it happen.

Developments occurred so fast that not even the most contemporary racer could keep abreast at all times. What was the "hot setup" one day was a tenth or two off the pace the following week. The Ramchargers racked up 9.82/145 times at Toledo while testing the new fuel injection; nitromethane fuel became commonly used after the MoPar injection was installed; and the Ford ban, which had been temporarily and provisionally lifted in April because team drivers were unable to get match races, was reinstated because of the opposition's fuel injection.

Then, by early summer, some Ford drivers, like Dick Brannan, rebuilt their Mustangs with altered wheelbases and fuel injection just like those on the MoPars they had been so incensed about! The ban was on-again/off-again as MoPars introduced nitro, Comets did the same, and Fords remained on gasoline.

Nicholson survived the crises best among the Comet-Mustang drivers. Employing the knowledge many years had given him, he quickly went with the wildest setup himself after a Springnationals A/FX win in 10.80 seconds. He knew he could not sell high ten-second performance to strip promoters any longer — not when the hemis were nearly a full second quicker.

Arnie Beswick, who also had a factory Merc in addition to his independent Pontiacs, won the Daytona Winternationals, but not in the Comet. It was shelved in favor of his blown GTO (and was removed from his operation not long afterward!).

Radical FX cars sprang up like weeds across the country as word got out that there was $500 to be made for a three-race match twice a week. Chevrolet and Pontiac fans were not left out of the 1965 excitement. Pete Seaton, son of a GM executive, latched on to a '66 prototype 427 Chevy engine and Turbo-Hydro transmission for use in a '65 Chevelle shell. Fiberglass, plexiglass, and a gutted interior, removal of a radiator and installation of a water reservoir in the trunk produced a total weight of 2800 pounds with 55 percent on the rear wheels. First run results were 10.07/140.18 on 25 percent nitro.

Tom Sturm enlarged his 427 to 454 cubic inches, shifted the wheelbase of a Chevelle around, and turned midtens. Beswick's gutted GTO, with blown 421 Pontiac power, led the independent assault with 9.70's in the resin. Doug Thorley fashioned a 2000-pound Chevy II with 98-inch wheelbase and 480-cubic-inch injected engine.

THE FIRST "EIGHT"

MoPars, led by veteran team members, continued in the bright lights despite this competition. Jim Thornton made history on August 7 when he broke the lights at 8.91 seconds with the Ramchargers' thoroughly lightened, fuel burning AWB Dodge. It was the first sub-nine-second run by an unblown stock-bodied car, albeit on a heavy nitro load.

Al Eckstrand, in a Plymouth, and Landy met in the Super Stock Nationals Unlimited class finals, closing out a test of nearly every top FX/funny car in the sport. The lawyer won this match of injected, fuel burning MoPars 9.70 to 9.52 with a hole shot on the Californian.

This win was overshadowed, however, by the sensational 9.32/146.57 time turned in by Bob Harrop in winning Heads-Up Eliminator from Bud Faubel. The New Jersey Dodge went to a risky 70 percent nitro, got a good trip on the resined strip, and came up with the best competition time to date by an unblown full-bodied car.

The Ramchargers took the Detroit World Championship Exhibition Eliminator purse in 10.31/135.12, and comrade-in-arms Sox owned low e.t. of 10.10. Faubel came up Unlimited winner at the *Cars* magaxine FX Championship in his AWB Dodge, going 9.85/138.46 for the win. Sox took the 3000-pound class, Bill Jenkins the 3200-pound in another Plymouth, and Thornton the hot 2700-pound bracket at 10.02/135.13.

Rules varied from race to race, and so did resulting performance, for the many FX cars could be adjusted to weigh anywhere from 2000 to 3400 pounds, although legitimate FX racing within NHRA rules was still Ford. Les Ritchey won a Nationals showdown from Covina, California, teammate Gas Ronda in a pairing of ohc Mustangs, resulting in 10.67- and 10.63-second times. Darrell Droke showed the B/FX form that put his rare '65 ohc Fairlane on top. He and Jerry Harvey, in another B/FX entry, marched through many events of the year, as did Bill Hoefer, in a C/FX Galaxie. Hoefer struck it rich at the Springnationals with a Junior Stock Eliminator triumph.

Blowers were the vogue by fall, boosting the power of Don Gay's Pontiac, Mr. Norm's Dodge, Tom McEwen's "Hemi-Cuda" (a rear-engine Hemi-Barracuda), Dick Branstner's "Dart Charger," and other headliners. The competition became so fierce that Jay Howell's August 173-mph speed with the rear-engine Dart Charger, which made his the first stock-bodied car to pass 170, was upstaged in November when Gary Dyer shook FX/funny car fans with an 8.63-second run. He sped Mr. Norm's blown Chicago Dodge, a completely gutted, windowless version, to the new low e.t. at Lions Drag Strip.

McEwen did 8.80/171 in the 'Cuda, Gay's

Pontiac was good for 9.20, and Beswick had many
8.90's at the time. Nicholson and Proffitt, in injected Comets, struggled at 9.50, as did Malcolm
Durham in his AWB Chevelle. Landy in an unblown Dodge, and dozens of other outstanding
FXers who were soon to turn to ultra-funny cars.

By 1966 the fastest FX/funny cars had left
the realm of Factory Experimental classification
and were genuine funny cars in the sense they are
known today. The special tube frames, rear-engine
locations, superchargers, and all were beyond even
the FX boundaries.

**Mickey Thompson's efforts to match Chrysler's hemi head
engine in 1964 produced a Ford of exotic proportion. Aluminum heads with outsized rocker arm framework and cross-
ram, dual four-barrel manifold on 427 were tried in a Thunderbolt, but were not especially impressive, particularly in view
of their exorbitant cost.**

FX LOSES IDENTITY WITH XS

Competition continued, however, for the FX cars, as new Experimental Stock (XS) classes enveloped the funnies. Darrell Droke outpowered Shirley Shahan's converted Plymouth Super Stock (now with injectors, ram tubes, slicks, etc.) with his special Fairlane at the AHRA Winternationals to become Mr. Stock Eliminator. The Downey, California, engine expert hustled to 10.64/130.81 in the B/FX-type overhead cammer.

Young Hank Taylor jumped into A/FX circles in 1964-65 with Hayden Proffitt machines, including this aluminum front end hemi Plymouth with the fender warning—"Tender Fender, Keep Off!"

Top: Bill "Maverick" Golden, now a wheelie star, led a MoPar assault on West Coast strips during the early 1960s. His "taxi yellow" '63 made SS/A or A/FX with a lightweight front end and flimsy front bumper, and the new 426 engine held a dozen records.

Bottom: The "Melrose Missile IV," a wicked new Plymouth from Oakland, was one of the strong and varied field that Dave Strickler shut down for 1963 Nationals A/FX honors. When the cream of the crop met under legal conditions, Chevy maintained its high performance with its last purpose-built race car—the Z-11 427. Forty thousand fans roared approval of the Chevy's 120 mph performance.

Top: A/FX action at the '63 Nationals included this face-off between Arlen Vanke's 421 Tempest and the fiberglass Ford of Emmett Austin. Class honors went to Dave Strickler's Chevy though, in 12.10/120.16.
Bottom: One of the most memorable FX races of all time was this one between Arnie Beswick and Don Nicholson. The aluminum 421 Pontiac and the 409 Chevy were crowd favorites known as two of the very quickest and most colorful match racers. Ironically, both drivers were disqualified, Beswick for not driving the car to the starting line himself, and Nicholson for drawing a red light on the single run! (Note the extreme up-down angle of the Chevy—the style in those days).

Super Stock Eliminator, also a misnomer, was Les Ritchey in his new A/FX Mustang, edging Tom Grove's Mustang. A 10.44/135.13 by Ford's coordinator of West Coast drag racing activities won the bucks. Ritchey also held the NHRA A/FX record with his 3200-pound stormer before a freak accident at Fontana Raceway resulted in fatal injuries to the popular veteran.

FX machines were slotted into Street Eliminator for the first time at NHRA's 1966 Winternationals, and turned the bracket into a rout. Jerry Harvey, from Indianapolis, marched through A/FX with a 10.64 ohc Mustang and Mike Schmitt, perennial handicap system standout, won B/FX at 11.66/123 in his '66 ohc Galaxie. The pair met in the bracket final after topping twenty other class winners; Harvey emerged with the crown.

Schmitt and Ed Terry, both from Northern California, then swept B/FX and C/FX classes in 427 and Cobra 289 Galaxies at both the Springnationals and the Nationals, racing under the once-again controlled rules, now similar to pre-1964. Schmitt parlayed his class win all the way to the Bristol Street Eliminator title, using effortless 11.85/119.68 times under the handicap system.

A number of new faces on the FX scene materialized from the Grand Stock Circuit that NASCAR's Drag Division scheduled on the East Coast. Melvin Yow, a Southerner with a swift hemi Dodge, won the circuit's points race and some $9000 in NASCAR competition.

The circuit continued in 1967, making up somewhat for a reduction in FX emphasis by NHRA that actually included discontinuance of FX classes in favor of the lower funny car classifications (XS). After a season of heated battle Dan Smoker, from Newport News, Virginia, won the Grand Stock Championship and a final bonus jackpot of $5000 with his hemi Plymouth. Close contenders included Tom Sneden, in a Dodge; Al Joniec, ohc Mustang; and Pee Wee Wallace with another strong Plymouth.

There was indeed plenty of open competition, but the match races that made FX driving lucrative for all a year and two years before were a thing of the past.

Among other accomplishments by cars that would formerly have been classed Factory Experimental were Springnationals C/XS and D/XS wins by Harvey's Mustang and Lee Smith's Illinois Plymouth, and World Series S/S Eliminator victory of Jack Thomas' '67 Dodge under "3200-pounds and carbs" rules. Harvey held both C/XS and D/XS NHRA National records at the end of the year.

A further decrease in FX interest by NHRA produced only S/XS class for blown fuel funny cars near 2000 pounds, and A/XS for unblown versions above 2600 pounds as 1968 possibilities. All of the more traditional FX cars were left the options of moving to Modified Production, Altered, or Gas competition with a few revisions to the cars.

The brief, but wonderfully colorful, era of Factory Experimental racing was over.

Top: A famous and controversial race. Bill Flynn's early lead over Arnie Beswick in 1964 Nationals A/MP final was soon lost. However, faulty win lights flashed in Flynn's lane and he was declared winner.
Bottom: This Texas E/MP features hood scoop, mag-type wheels, open headers, new cam, and panel wagon style in effort to win with 265 engine.

4

Modified Production

One class bracket created especially for the thousands of drivers of streetworthy modified cars is a real "sleeper" in Street Eliminator competition. NHRA Modified Production classes, six in all, present the finest opportunity for modified stock cars to race their big brothers on an even basis by handicap. AHRA's Sportsman category among its many hot rod sections most closely parallels Modified Production (MP) in rules, though not entirely, and provides many of the same benefits for modern street rods.

Street machines with hood scoops, mag wheels, bored out engines, and multiple carburetion are right at home in Modified Production. They wouldn't fit in Super Stock, and wouldn't stand a chance if matched heads-up against the totally "built" gas coupes — which is exactly why rulesmakers established the bracket in 1964.

Until that time gassers were pretty much "streetable," as the rules required. Legal headlights, nearly stock suspensions, upholstered interiors with full dashboards, standard size radiators, and carburetors were still common, enabling most of the gassers to double as mean-looking drive-in buggies during the week. They blossomed in a hurry then, and before long were as far from being street-legal as dragsters. Rules changed and racers pressed their advantage until blown Chrysler engines in ultra-light fiberglass Willys were the norm.

Even in the lower gas classes a '67 Chevy with popular 301-cubic-inch 283-type engine, or '54 Ford boasting a new 427 engine, or newer models with speed equipment manifold and carburetors stood no chance against seriously constructed race cars and, as a result, the backbone of the sport was weakened. The rodder — that Weekend Warrior — had no place to race. Gas classes were too professional; and the stimulation and self-satisfaction of reworking the factories' offerings couldn't be found in the stock classes.

MODIFIEDS — THE GASSERS OF OLD

The Modified Production rules were therefore made very similar to the earlier gas coupe statutes. That is, they allowed a fairly free hand in modifying, but prevented the all-out competition car that was unsuitable for actual street driving. Most important, full street equipment in working hook-up — lights, horn, generator, windshield wipers, starter, water pump, fan, etc. — became mandatory. Full bodies and upholstery were required. Nonfactory fiberglass and aluminum panels, and plexiglass windows were prohibited.

Chassis work was limited to FX-type improvements like traction bars. The radical straight-axle replacements and wheelbase alterations that signalled the gassers' trip into orbit were strictly prohibited. Level car attitude, stock engine location, and 100-inch minimum wheelbase requirements were established, and there was a rule limiting tires to cheater slicks.

Most MP experimenting was done under the hood. Any production engine in any American chassis provided about as much latitude as anyone could use. Carburetion was one of the stiff restrictions, and a limit of dual four-barrel or three two-barrel systems made multiple units like six Strombergs, fuel injection, superchargers, and the like, taboo.

Wild cams, stroker kits, ported heads, custom pistons, and other internal parts came under no scrutiny, so it was possible for a budget racer to build his own engine to at least the potential of late model engine swaps into early bodies.

In summary, the MP classes encouraged engine modification to whatever degree one could afford or could enjoy on the street, and applied a gentle restraint on body/chassis alteration to retain their street/strip purpose.

Weight-per-cubic-inch factors determined MP classes just as in gas coupes and other nonstock brackets. The initial divisions for 1964 were: A/MP — 7.00 to 8.99 pounds per cubic inch; B — 9.00–10.99; C — 11.00–12.99; D — 13.00 and more for late V8 engines and E/MP — 7.00–10.99; F/MP — 11.00 and more for unblown flathead V8's, six-cylinder and straight eight engines with stock-type heads, and opposed sixes (like Corvairs) and pre-1960 four-cylinder engines with any type heads. This equitable breakdown underwent several minor revisions as individual popularity, new cars, and records demanded, resulting in a more streamlined slate for 1968.

Careful study of the potential winners in Modified Production soon produced a pattern of success through all the classes, topped by late model hemi MoPars in A/MP. The Super Stock and Factory Experimental Plymouths and Dodges made the 7.00 class bottom of 3000 pounds for 426 inches when lightened 300 to 400 pounds for match racing; A/MP became a handy slot when legal NHRA racing came due.

In addition, many of the Super Stocks of the previous year or two, no longer legal or competitive in the class, moved to A/MP even though they did not utilize the full extent of permitted modification.

B/MP was a haven for heavy steel-bodied entries with 400-plus-cubic-inch Chevy, Ford, Pontiac, or MoPar engines. They had to weigh 3850 pounds to make "B," without illegal ballast and with less than 500 pounds of legally installed extra weight. Lightweight models were therefore not eligible, leaving the class to the fully loaded street machines.

Standard engine/body combinations such as the 327 Chevy fit right into C/MP at 3400 to 3600 pounds, as did strong V8 compacts like 289 Ford Fairlanes, 283 Chevy IIs, and 273 Darts, along with older conversions including 283–301 Chevys in '55–'57 bodies at 3200 pounds.

High-winding small engines in heavy stock bodies made up D/MP. At 13.00 pounds per cubic inch even the 265 Chevy V8 had to scale 3450, so any year shell made the bracket, but 289 Ford and 273 MoPars were about as big as one could go.

Modern six-cylinder mills, including the slant six Chrysler, and Chevy and Ford versions, showed their big valve, high efficiency strength in E and F/MP, completely outclassing flatheads, older model sixes, and straight eights.

BRACKET HEROES STAND OUT

Among national leaders of A/MP from 1964 to the present have been Bill "Maverick" Golden, Bill Flynn, Robert Nance, Bill Jenkins, Dick Landy, Gene Kidder, and other notables whose match machines were perfectly suited to the rules. "Maverick" powered an early 123.65-mph national record with his "taxicab" Dodge; Flynn, then an unknown from New Haven, Connecticut, won the '64 Nationals class at 11.95/119.36; and Jenkins won the '65 class in his versatile Plymouth hemi with much improved 11.10/130.24 times.

Nance, a Ringgold, Georgia, veteran of stock car modification, held the class record for much of the first two years on an 11.11/129.27 with his Plymouth. Landy shone in A/MP with one of his five 1968 Winternationals Dodge entries, ringing up strong 10.89/130.81 clockings. His 426 Charger was subtly modified to fit both AHRA and NHRA rules.

Joining Flynn in the '64 winner's circle were Bill Hoefer, who later went on to win the World

Street Eliminator Championship in his D/MP '56 Chevy; Ralph Holloman's Kentucky C/MP '57 Chevy, which almost won the Nationals Eliminator title after three tough rounds; and Pete McNicholl, who continued to dominate E and F/MP for several years afterward. Hoefer, from Covina, California, held the D/MP national mark of 12.92/108.04 into 1965.

In addition to the small V8 NHRA winners like Hoefer and Holloman, another interesting driver/car team was active in AHRA's Sportsman bracket. Jim Tice, president of the association, held the 1963 I/SM record with a 14.90/98.03 timing of his slippery '51 Studebaker coupe.

An E/MP '54 Corvette of Earl Britt, Sioux Falls, South Dakota, came to the fore at 99.85 mph, and McNicholl's six-cylinder Dart ruled F/MP with an e.t. of 13.88 seconds. These six-hole classes became very popular for drivers of the Chrysler slant-six products. The factory's wild Hyper-Pak option put them out in front, capable of setting and maintaining records for their advantage in Eliminator competition against other classes. Ron Root, a former policeman (now director of NHRA's Charter Club program), shifted his "Gendarme" Dart to national prominence as 1964 Winternationals Street Eliminator, and others joined the fray.

The factory made the first "six" hop-up package available after Daytona introduction of the Hyper-Pak. With a 276-degree cam with stiff valve springs, V8 size exhaust system with split headers, four-barrel carburetion, and heavy duty clutch, the

225-inch six had up to 190 horsepower and a winning reputation.

Britt's E/MP Chevy six, turned F/MP under 1968 rules, was a top national contender from the first. Most recently it won the '67 Winternationals, Springnationals, and National Championship classes, nearly took the World crown in Tulsa, then repeated at the '68 Winternationals.

Britt used a 334-cubic-inch six in a 2715-pound '54 Corvette that he converted after his wife had used it daily. All modifications were of high quality, yet were not wastefully expensive. Among the custom equipment items were: Kay Sissell reworked heads and valves; Sissell intake manifold with triple Weber carburetors; and Moon MR–5 cam with extreme .566-inch lift and 330-degree duration. Britt chose a '66 Chevy Turbo-Hydro transmission to obtain the consistency that wins in Eliminator action, and 4.56 gears with cheater slicks. His record best with this combination was 12.55/110.

Pete Gardner also proved that new Chevy sixes could reach the top. He led the East Coast NHRA points chase and established the 1967 E/MP national mark of 108.83 mph with his '65 Chevy/Falcon.

Ralph Ridgeway's 11.89-second '55 Chevy C/MP champ, and Richard Wood's '56 Chevy D/-MP station wagon led their divisions during 1967, with Wood rising to Winternational Street Eliminator status. His Fremont, California, entry hit steady 12.80's en route to a $4000 jackpot, and although he also got his class(E/MP) in the 1968 event, Wood's bid for the repeat money fell short.

Small V8's have proven popular in these middle MP classes where 289 Fords, 283 Chevys, and 273 MoPars can duel to the death. Most Chevy models are light '55–'57 bodies and newer small-block engines, with a few Chevy II's involved. Ford fans use the late Falcon and Fairlane bodies; MoPar hopefuls, the Darts and Barracudas.

BUILDING AN MP ENTRY

Typical preparation of the late model street/strip machine according to Modified Production standards is similar to that of Duncan-Haas' 1965 Dodge Dart. Their "Yellow Jacket" 273 got a prerace treatment which led to 13.00/108 performance as an AHRA Formula 5 H/Stock Optional (!) and NHRA C/MP.

Engine blueprinting was complemented by the addition of aluminum rods, 12.5 to 1 pistons, and Racer Brown ST–14 camshaft. Heads were carefully matched for the legal maximum 57.3cc per cylinder. Headers, ignition adjustment, and alternating single and dual four-barrel carb systems (according to the rules) were the extent of the modifications to the engine.

Chassis work included the installation of a big Dodge third member with axles, etc., and a 5.12 gear set. Heavy duty shocks, mag wheels, and cheater slicks — just like a stocker setup — resulted in a moderate but successful MP example that provided numerous wins and a lot of fun on Western strips.

Ron Root and Don McCain amazed West Coast Modified fans and racers with a '65 Mustang capable of 12.50/111 performance. Initially the car ran with a single four-barrel, but was greatly modified after success in AHRA Formula 5 G/SO (!) and elapsed time brackets.

The construction and racing of a modified stocker in 1968 were subject to several changes in rules and a shift in the class breakdowns that deserved attention before any serious work was done — or any hard-earned cash spent.

The battery, presumably relocated in the trunk, could weigh no more than 100 pounds. Previous wording of the applicable rule had put no limit on this important weight transfer, and commercial units of several hundred pounds were often found serving as extraordinary ballast and traction aid in MP cars.

Hand-in-hand with the battery rule was the notation that no MP could be more than 500 pounds over its original shipping weight in order to make a lower class than it ordinarily would join. This practical safety limit was set because brakes and handling are seriously affected by too much more than stock weight. The flexibility of classes for some racers may have been impaired, but elimination of the rear-heavy lead barges made MP safer and more interesting.

Newer models with factory-installed fiberglass or aluminum bodies, i.e., the SS-FX converts to MP, were required to have roll bars built in, and this meant another 30 to 40 pounds of weight had to be shaved off to reach the class minimum. A new muffler stipulation placed an eighteen-inch minimum length on the lightweight replacements commonly used, preventing a trend to ultra-light shorties that were not legal street-use mufflers.

The A/MP's could now mount slicks via the same rule that allows FX cars any tire/wheel combination that will fit into the wheel well, but the modifieds were granted an important additional concession — wheel wells could be radiused (enlarged) as long as the edges were rolled under and they retained their original shape. Conversion bodies with late model power which could not otherwise accommodate necessarily large tires were thus made competitive with new FX-types when fitted with giant slicks.

Lower MP classes were not permitted such luxury, but were a step ahead of the early rules which put tread-width maximums on tires per size; for example, 5.5 inches for any tire of 6.00 to 6.70 x 15 size. The 1968 rules permitted cheater slick width of seven inches regardless of size.

One additional benefit to cars that could use it was a reduction in the wheelbase minimum from 100 to 98 inches. Corvettes became eligible, along with a few other small cars whose traction would be an advantage.

Many regular competitors found their cars in different classes when the new season opened, for NHRA weight-per-cubic-inch breaks were revised. Only one class, F/MP, was set aside for flatheads, sixes, etc., leaving five for the more conventional entries. Integrals of 1.49 were added to the 7.00 pounds-per-cubic-inch. A/MP minimum in making the new scale, so that B/MP, for instance, was 8.50 to 9.99 pounds-per-cubic-inch and E/MP was 13.00 and up — the former "D" area. Flatheads that formerly had had an 8.00 minimum ratio, were now bottomed at 9.00. These class breaks remained unchanged for 1969.

Because the Modified Production rules were comparatively liberal, and because moderate weight adjustments were permitted in the bracket, the new classes did not change the list of "most eligible" cars, but simply required a little more or less preparation to best fit the new ratio ranges. A '57 Chevy of 3400 pounds with 283 engine would now have to take off only 125 pounds instead of 285 to be legally at its lightest for D/MP. Of course, inasmuch as the bracket was based on cubic inches instead of horsepower, engines would still have to be as strong as rules permit, regardless of weight changes.

Modified Production continues to be a bracket from which serious racers can enter lucrative Street Eliminator competition using "easy" records, while at the same time acting as a legal stomping ground for nearly every modified street machine that growls through town during the week. Quite an attractive makeup.

The Chevy gasser pilot with the unlikely name of Ferd Napfel achieved a record including the 1967 national F/G record of 107.61 mph, runner-up finish to Deloy Naeb, 1966 World Street Elim Champion, class wins at many big meets, and a popular running battle with East Coast rival Clyde Seigle.

5

Gas Coupes

Construction of the first drag strips during the late 1940's came none too soon for the needs of postwar high-performance enthusiasts — the hot rodders. They had developed the science of street racing to the point that big engines in small bodies were required to earn any "tough reputation." New cars from Detroit could not stand up to those with modifications, so modifications it had to be.

Early Fords — most popularly the '32–'34 and '39–'40 models — and some Chevrolets — ruled when they were powered by hot flathead Ford-Merc engines. It was the desire to be the best that resulted in the appearance of street rods that local citizens found unacceptable.

The organized strips incorporated into their rules a place for gas coupes and sedans. All-out race cars had their bracket, fuel-burning entries theirs, and the fendered street machines had the gas classes. NHRA rules for 1954 competition provided A through D/Gas divisions of 0 to 8.5 pounds-per-cubic-inch; 8.6 to 10.5; 10.6 to 12.5;

and 12.6 and up in the first official breakdown which permitted uniform national classification. All street equipment, including starter, lights, and exhaust system, was made mandatory, and certain stipulations were set forth that the gas coupes be fully fendered and upholstered, i.e., nearly stock and ready for legal street use.

EARLY WINNERS ON THE COAST

West Coast racers had the advantages of a few years' experience and the convenience of being close to nearly every speed equipment manufacturer, so it is not surprising that their times led the bracket. Pacesetters such as Gene Adams, Howard Johansen, Doug Cook earned fearsome notoriety and came up against East Coast opposition for the first time at the 1955 NHRA National Championships.

Not all the big iron from either coast could tow to Grand Bend, Kansas, of course, because the prizes were minimal, but honors were split geographically. Dick Cadwallader, a Pennsylvanian, hit 96.87 mph in winning A/G with his '54 Olds engine/'33 Ford coupe. Johansen, wheeling the '55 Chevy that had served as a test car for his father's camshaft firm, stood out as C/G winner with speeds as high as 99.88 mph.

Adams became a national symbol of gasser supremacy at the same time as a result of continuing Engle Racing Cams' magazine ads which reported his record-setting exploits. His '50 Olds coupe, a 4100-pound heavyweight in opposition to the light early bodies, rang up speeds of 106 mph by 1955.

Also strong in an Olds gasser were Masters-Richter, a duo later famous in fuel dragster circles. Their '56 Santa Ana clocking of 107.92 split the "fastest Olds" picture. Texan John Lovelean showed the heavyweights the answer at the Nationals, however, winning A/G with a McCullough-blown '53 Buick/'34 Ford tudor sedan combination. His 109.89 was 11 mph faster than the '55 winner in this era which placed no emphasis on elapsed times.

Many gas coupes got new Chevy engines after the introduction of the '55 V8, and while Cad-Olds devotees filled the upper classes, much of the bracket's increasing popularity was due to the light, available, comparatively inexpensive Chevy engines.

In a search for the most equitable set, the sanctioning bodies changed classes from year to year, resting for 1956 with weight/displacement breaks of: A/G — 0 to 10.59; B — 10.60 to 12.59; C — 12.60 to 14.59; D — 14.60 and up. A blower moved any car up to the next higher class.

The 1957–58 period was a temporary peak in gas coupe interest, for after '59, Super Stocks right off the showroom floor came along to outperform many gassers, and participation in all but the top classes began to subside. It was just the beginning of a colorful era, however, and the few dozen most impressive racers earned not only a great following, but eventually high-priced match races that brought about some of the radical A/GS modifications of the 1960's.

Adams continued his well-publicized big numbers, but remained in B/G with the Olds, which now had a '57 engine of 370 cubic inches and a blower, and used a pair of heavy manhole covers in the trunk to make the class weight. A traditional '37 Cad-LaSalle three-speed floor shift, pressure fuel tank mounted next to the driver, and Traction Masters were parts of Adams' winning setup, as was an exclusive exhaust system which had been modified to a four-port configuration with dump tubes of about 36-inch length. This was the fastback with stock radiator and front end, full upholstery and dashboard, steel wheels, and recap slicks that set a new B/G record of 111.24 mph at the '57 Nationals.

Glen Ward, another notable California dragster pilot who entered racing with a gas coupe, set the "A" mark at the same meet — but was only .70 mph faster than the speedy Olds with a 386-cubic-inch Cad/'33 Ford. Class winners were a surprising group of Texas entries, topped by H. L. Lawhon's '55 Olds/'33 Ford that took A/G at 13.14/96.25.

BIG GUNS LET LOOSE

The competitive gas classes picked up more momentum, and the likes of Doug Cook, Ed Schartman, and Dick Harryman took up the cause. Cook began his decade-long rampage in the bracket with a B/G '37 Chevy coupe (and Howard cam, adding to the camshaft grinders' heated rivalry). He matched Adams' 111 record at Lions

Drag Strip in 12.48 seconds during 1958, using a 299-inch Chevy engine. Harryman and John Mazmanian, also from Los Angeles, ran an Adams-type B/G Olds to 107.36 at Santa Ana. And Schartman, who later went to Super Stocks and now drives a 190-mph funny Comet, opened some eyes on the East Coast by taking Daytona Winternationals B/G money with a 104.37-mph '56 Chevy. It had been enlarged to 4 x 3⅜ inches, but was otherwise quite stock!

George Montgomery, not to become "Ohio George" until the mid-'60s, had emerged as one of the Midwest's finest. His lowered '34 Ford coupe boasted a hot 415-cubic-inch Cad engine with 11 to 1 compression, dual coils, four carbs. A LaSalle transmission, 4.44 gears, and small 7.10 x 15 slicks took him to 115 mph and consistent wins.

The 1958 Nationals offered all the big machinery a chance to settle gasser differences — and who came out from B/G to become NHRA's first Little Eliminator but Junior Thompson in a blown Chevy/'41 Studebaker, the first of its kind. Thompson led the way to extreme body and engine height with this car, elevating the works well above the chassis for maximum weight transfer to the rear wheels, and prompting NHRA to adopt a new rule regarding the maximum engine height. Crankshafts were henceforth to be no more than twenty-four inches above the ground.

Still another current gasser star, K. S. Pittman, came on later in the year with a 12.43/114.95 timing in Harryman's 4300-pound Olds.

This pattern of early participation, experimentation, and success by today's gas coupe contingent — Cook, Mazmanian, Pittman, Montgomery, Thompson, and others who moved to different machines — is considerably different from the history of dragsters. Only a few drivers of the current leading rails — like Garlits and Karamesines — were winners ten or more years ago. Don Prudhomme, Tom Ivo, Connie Kalitta, Pete Robinson were not yet prominent, and such contemporary stars as Dave Beebe, Tom McEwen, AA/FD recordholders Jim and Alison Lee, Hank Westmoreland, Billy Scott, Mike Snively, Jerry Ruth were yet to enter the picture. Art Chrisman, Setto Postoian, the Bean Bandits, Cook & Bedwell, Nationals Top Eliminators Calvin Rice, Mel Heath, Buddy Sampson, Ted Cyr, Rodney Singer, Leonard Harris — none are found in the rails of today.

The accumulated experience of today's gas coupe contingent has made this small handful almost unbeatable in AA/G (formerly A/Gas Supercharged). Several hopefuls have attempted to jump into the fray with blown gassers "out the box," built by knowledgeable firms with no expense spared, but their fate has been discouraging.

K. S. Pittman debuted the Pittman-Edwards blown Olds/'40 Willys B/Gasser in 1959, bumping the pace to 11.65/121.29 at 3400 pounds, and shortly afterwards Montgomery began a streak of Nationals class wins that would defy his nationwide rivals. He drove his Cad-powered '33 Willys all the way to Little Eliminator, and repeated the feat in 1960 with sizzling 11.53/130.57 times.

The money run of the Eliminator brought the

Willys and Texan Don Breithaupt's "DCB" coupe together, but only after two false starts (which were permitted during those years) did Montgomery pull it off.

Other gas coupe successes included Doug "Cookie" Cook's C/GS class win and national record of 120.16 mph in the Howard Cams Spl. '40 Willys, and the first of Johnny Loper's big wins, a B/G runnerup to Street Eliminator.

Tom Sturm had joined the B/G battle on the Coast, Ollie Olsen was storming Florida in his Chevy/Henry J, and Mike "Mad Russian" Marinoff campaigned the screaming C/G '55 Chevy from Milwaukee.

Cook teamed up with owners Tim Woods and Fred Stone for the '61 season, springing the original Stone-Woods-Cook machine on Winternationals opposition and outperforming the field at 11.22/126.93. The blown Olds/'40 Willys B/GS times were even better than those of the A/GS winner Joe Pisano — a forecast of things to come. John Loper towed over from Phoenix, Arizona, for B/G and Street Eliminator laurels with the same 301-inch Chevy/'41 Willys that had nearly captured the previous Nationals.

Records fell as speed equipment improved and gas coupe maximum performance combinations of chassis, tires, drive line, and engine became popular. Sounder engineering produced national marks led by S-W-C's A/GS 11.11/127.04. The Grist Brothers of California were unusual with an enormous Edsel engine in their by-now-standard Willys body, and held the A/G record of 118.89

mph, but the rest of the class leaders were Chevy-powered machines from Ohio.

Ed Schartman, Ron Hassell, and the Hrudka Brothers set B, C, D/G marks. Six-cylinder cars followed Pete McNicholl's G/G 183-inch Valiant power.

A Kentucky B/G Chevy/Willys upset the big names at the '61 Nationals, but week-to-week competition produced the same slate of winners across the nation. The surprise was Junior Garrison's NHRA Street Eliminator victory for the big prize of the year. He drove a new Pontiac home after 12.42/112.60 performance.

Ollie Olsen's immaculate new A/G threat, a Chevy/'40 Willys with unique, intricate rear suspension designed by the Florida veteran, swept its class in 11.68/120.64. In tune with the latest gas coupe methods, Olsen's winner was built with lightened front axle, disc brakes, cut down radiator, drilled front wheels (instead of magnesium), trunk-mounted battery, a stark interior fashioned from sheet aluminum, and fat M & H slicks.

NEW RULES DROP TIMES

One of the important formative years of gas coupe development was 1962. Rules were liberalized to allow plexiglass windows, etc., and dedicated gas racers became even more serious about the problem of going faster. S-W-C again headed the big numbers, culminating in the first nine-second time by any gas coupe, a 9.66/144.95 October charge at San Gabriel Drag Strip. This fantastic performance was far from the norm, though, despite the considerable overall improvement. Montgomery, for instance, hit a 10.48 best, and Cook's winning A/GS times at the Nationals were 10.59/136.77.

Another big effort put the Moody-Jones C/GS Chevy coupe in the Street Eliminator winner's slot at 12.09/110.12. Loper's "B" and a strange

A gas class embarrassment: This injected Mustang, converted to AHRA gas coupe specs, lost its right rear wheel during acceleration, and drove off the strip.

newcomer, the heavy E/G Chevy/'49 Packard of Dave Koffel, also achieved Nationals glory.

Mike Marinoff rang up a scorching B/GS 10.88/128.57 after stuffing his Chevy in a Willys, the Grists' 11.61/121.45 held national A/G stature, and the Airoso Brothers from Tulare, California, topped B/G by virtue of a 12.01 by their 294-inch DeSoto/Willys.

Ron Colson, still a Chevy booster in 1968 in AA/GD, was embarrassing the official B/G 12.01 with 11.33/131.78 luster, driving the Colson-Wood injected Chevy/'41 Stude from Illinois.

Gas coupe competition by this time had been centered almost entirely in four areas of the country, flourishing despite a turn in the attention of most regions to fuel dragsters and Super Stocks. California, Texas, Ohio-Indiana, and scattered regions of the East including Florida supported the bracket. Racers from these areas held most of the records and made up the entry of national meets.

The Los Angeles Stone, Woods, and Cook group, combining the racing knowledge of Doug Cook and the finances of building contractor Tim Woods, virtually owned the gas coupe division as 1963 unfolded. They held both A/GS and B/GS official records, swept to the Winternationals Middle Eliminator crown in 10.02/139.96, and won regular match races on western strips. Other Californians shared the Pomona limelight in a big gasser show that found Dick Bourgeois netting Little Eliminator with a Chevy/Fiat 11.35/124.30, and K. S. Pittman routing B/GS in his 11.08/122.61 fiberglass Willys.

Top: "Down South" D/Gasser of the Mullinax Brothers and Owens is a '55 Chevy with all the popular gasser modifications: light front end, straight front axle drilled to save weight, wide reversed chrome wheels and big slicks, single bucket seat interior, and small block Chevy power, producing hot 12-second times during '67 action.

Bottom: In 1968 the "look" of gas coupe racing began to change as more and more competitors were building gassers based on something other than the almost-standard Willys or Austin body. Fred Hurst drove this injected, hemi-powered Barracuda .06 seconds under the national A/Gas record to capture Street Eliminator honors at the NHRA World Finals in Tulsa, Oklahoma.

Eastern stars now included Gene Altizer, an A/G standout from Arlington, Virginia. He helped to bring the diminutive Anglia body to prominence by setting the 10.97-second class record, and by going all the way to a close final run for Middle Eliminator at the Nationals. Predictably, it was Montgomery's Willys, now with a Chevy engine, that beat Altizer for the bucks. Ohio's pride had established a tradition by this time that perplexed the competition — winning the big ones without having the quickest car.

The confrontation between West Coast hot dogs and the Indy classic crowd favorite from Dayton, Ohio, came to be an annual highlight of the meet. Montgomery gave up big claimed times, got down to mastering the Nationals track, and came away winner.

Rulesmakers countered the gas fraternity's ingenuity and possible overenthusiasm by raising the A/GS minimum weight to displacement ratio from 4.00 pounds per cubic inch to 5.00, curbing the plummetting times temporarily. But a little more power, better tires, and improved techniques had e.t.'s back down again before most people noticed the change.

STONE-WOODS-COOK VS. "BIG JOHN" MAZMANIAN

A new personality, "Big John" Mazmanian, successful Los Angeles rubbish contractor, threw a flashy new-blown Chrysler/Willys against class "kings" Stone-Woods-Cook, and with Bob "Bones" Balogh driving, proved that they were not invincible and that the added 5.00 weight was not hard to overcome. Cook won the '64 Winternationals class at 10.03/142.85, but "Big John" got Bakersfield satisfaction with a 9.77 e.t. that really established the car — the first Chrysler-hydro gas coupe.

The two "bucks-up" racers, Woods and Mazmanian, topped each other week after week, with S-W-C clocking 9.91/146.10 mph before mid-year, and "Bones-Big John" reaching heights of their own. Mazmanian's blown Chrysler with B & M hydro was the first such combination, and early showings convinced S-W-C that their Olds would have to go. The result was a nearly identical 2700-pound Willys with 450-inch early hemis, hydros, 4.56 gears, 11.00 x 15 slicks.

The only significant difference was in the camshaft, and on this point revolved a trade paper advertising campaign that kept them — and Montgomery — in the limelight. Stone, Woods, and Cook insisted in print that "Big John" was using an Engle cam, not the claimed Iskenderian, when his last record was set. He retaliated by stating that anyone could inspect his cam (for a price). Montgomery was accused of being the "Easter Bunny," so-called because it was claimed that he was hiding from West Coast cars throughout the year until his annual appearance at the Nationals. His stated Isky cam was also under mock fire.

Such comical publicity brought big fees for S-W-C versus "Big John" match races and later meetings with Montgomery, the first big money that gas coupes had ever earned.

The Nationals temporarily interrupted this game. A/GS was Montgomery's personal property it seemed, and "Ohio George" nipped Cook in a dramatic 10.20/138.68 before a cheering partisan crowd. K. S. Pittman sounded off his new Chrysler/'33 bear for a new 9.99/146 NHRA record, saving some face for the West Coast clan (though he was sponsored by S & S Parts of Falls Church, Virginia).

Montgomery's spotless '33, improved each year since its 1959 introduction, boasted a 374-inch blown Chevy with Isky cam and a fiberglass replica body that brought weight down to 2350 pounds. His attention to detail set the pale blue super apart with polished mag wheels, completely chromed undercarriage, aluminum sheet interior, and trap-door parachute box.

Other class winners included several racers that came to score heavily in following years. Jack Merkel's 10.54/134.53 B/GS entry from New York; Jim Lutz' A/G Anglia; Ron Hassell's B/G; Gene Moody's "D"; and Ferd Napfel's F/G — all Chevy-powered — were threats at every major meet.

In fact, Napfel, from Catonsville, Maryland, won the '65 Nationals Street Eliminator jackpot, and Moody, in his D-E/G Chevy from Bloomfield, Indiana, became World Street Eliminator Champion, edging Johnny Leibham's Texas C/GS challenge in the final.

Moody's car was typical of most successful

lower-class gas coupes, a '55 Chevy with radiused wheel wells that would accept big rubber. An injected '61 Chevy engine bored to 301 inches was set back in the chassis the 10 percent maximum of the wheelbase. Unique handiwork included a light '40 Ford axle assembly up front in place of the stock A-frames and coil springs.

An historic accomplishment nearly equal to Moody's World title win was the Jack Merkel Nationals A/GS win at the expense of "Ohio George," albeit as the result of a red light start. It marked the first time in years that anyone had unseated the Ohio Willys at the meet, and ironically it had been done with a blown 365-inch Chevy/'33 Willys nearly identical to Montgomery's — not with a monstrous Chrysler.

The Ridgewood, New York, entry used a similar glass front end and simple fiberglass bucket seat interior on a 100-inch wheelbase. Merkel chose a beefed hydro, coil rear springs, and Olds rear end. Front disc brakes, the smallest radiator ever seen, and bumper-mounted parachute were also employed on the giant-killer that earned a place in drag racing history that day.

A/G champ Lutz, from Minneapolis, took a radical approach with a tilt-front Anglia. The 375-inch Chevy with extreme 13.5 to 1 compression and four-speed transmission led to 10.82/131.96 records. A drilled frame, brief 90-inch wheelbase, Crosley front end with disc brakes, and Pontiac rear assembly were a more advanced combination than his competitors.

Earlier '65 winter action — the Winternationals

— gave Pittman a place in the sun. He rose to a thundering 9.87/145.86 A/GS class win over runnerup Cook's 9.93. The rugged hod carrier's Willys used a blown 420-inch Chrysler, B & M hydro, and giant 11.00 x 16 slicks.

MGM PENETRATES A/GS

One of the few new "A" superteams that have profitably penetrated A/GS also shone in 1965 in a winning streak that continued into the following year. Gene Ciambella's MGM-C & O Willys pick-up shocked older hands by upsetting the AHRA National Championships. John Loper also scored at the meet, and the Herrerra & Sons B/G Willys stormed to Street Eliminator over Barber-Greer's C/G hope.

The upstart MGM blown Chrysler matched the A/GS competition with fiberglass body, tube front end, heavily weighted rear pushbar-bumper, and the ultimate stretching of drag racing rules — a radiator no bigger than a cereal box. The concept of driving on the street has been distorted beyond practicality by all of the do-or-die "As."

Hotter in '66 than before, MGM overpowered Cook, "Big John," et al for A/GS honors at the AHRA and NHRA Winternationals, and the AHRA Nationals as well, smoking up 9.07/155 times at the latter! Ciambella's pickup was definitely a genuine new member of the gasser elite.

Pittman, Barber-Greer, the Kohler Brothers, and a new Junior Thompson Chrysler/Austin also rode high before midyear. K.S. earned an AHRA

Little Eliminator title; B-G the Street crown with their C/Gasser. Ed Kohler topped Johnny Loper for the Winternationals A/G class in a battle of Chevy/Anglias, and Thompson got by the Bakersfield A/GS entry with his all-out Austin.

Coming out of temporary retirement, Thompson obtained what he thought would be a topper for the Willys machines — a 1950 Austin. Given the from-the-ground-up treatment for ultimate A/GS competition, the Austin became a lightweight sizzler with blown 360-inch Chevy, then hemi Chrysler power. A glass body replaced the English original, and tube front axle, rear coil springs, narrowed Olds rear end à la dragster, and beefed hydro were installed.

"Ohio George," not one to miss an opportunity to improve his venerable '33 Willys, took the winter months to squeeze Ford's new overhead cam 427 between its fenders then await the Springnationals where the Willys hustled to nine-second wins. Several months later the new 1000-horsepower flyer once again repeated the AA/G Nationals ritual for Montgomery in 9.53/153.58.

This "assistance" by Ford, the success of the ohc in FoMoCo funny cars, and a trend-setting desire to achieve funny car crowd identification with a gas coupe prompted Montgomery to build the first late-model AA/G the following winter, showing at the '67 Springnationals with a 427 Mustang that had the pits buzzing. A stunning off-the-trailer time of 8.98 seconds answered any pessimists.

Mazmanian was busy on the Coast constructing

Top: This six-cylinder C/SR, held the class national record of 122.51 mph during 1967.
Middle: Two street roadsters streak for the finish line.
Bottom: EMPI Volkswagen pulls front wheels up on 1-2 shift! It uses modified VW engine with Okrasa heads, Weber carbs, etc. for H/G domination at 12.90/106!

a new chopped-top Austin to keep pace. Built like a funny car or altered with tubular body cage and custom rectangular tub chassis, the superlight AA/G transcended all of the original "stock body with engine conversion" intention of gas coupe classes. It lacked headlights, bumpers, workable windows, and other street necessities, but it did fit rules that had become nearly wide-open.

Streamlined glass and steel body enclosed a sophisticated suspension, an enormous '57 Chrysler, TorqueFlite automatic transmission, and narrow Pontiac rear end. This latest in Mazmanian's series also uncorked first-time 8.90's for driver Dick Bourgeoise.

Still another competitive new car was turning 8's for the Kohler Brothers. They completed the old Ford-Chrysler-Chevy rivalry with a 454-cubic-inch Chevy/Anglia. "King Kong" actually filled a void left in gasser racing when Stone-Woods-Cook went to a funny car — neglecting the famed "Swindler A." (Kohler's glass-bodied swifty is no less radical than Mazmanian's. It weighs only 2200 pounds with TorqueFlite, custom chassis work, weighted rear bumper, wheelie casters, and an antiseptically bare interior. NHRA rules prohibit the Anglia's 90-inch wheelbase in AA/G, however, so Kohler enters it in altered classes at national meets and runs it as a gasser in other events.)

In spite of such apparent progress in the gas coupe ranks, the '67 Nationals class winners were a familiar lot — Montgomery, Gene Moody, Ferd Napfel, Becker-O'Connell, and Empi-Dean Lowry. The glitter of dragster times by 'way out AA/G's, it seems, has affected the majority of classes very slightly.

A notable effort at the World Finals by Walt Marrs of Monrovia, California, also corroborated this fact; his old-style BB/G '40 Willys had been a Super Eliminator contender at many previous meets. This time the wailing Chevy was not only keeping pace, but was too strong and broke out of its .10-second-under-the-national-class-record limit in maintaining a handicap lead over charging Joe Davis, and was disqualified in the World Championship run.

LOWER CLASSES LOTS OF FUN

Admittedly, a lot of the glamor of the gas coupe division is carted away by the eye-opening blown entries, but more than a few owners have found their flathead and six-cylinder gassers rewarding. Dean Lowry's incredible Volkswagen is the most famous of the small-engine sprinters, having ruled H/G in national competition with astounding 12.80-second/106-mph VW performance.

The Empi VW became an instant hit with crowds because of its economy image and because of the enormous handicap lead it got from faster Street Eliminator cars, and it made a perfect project for the Riverside, California, sponsors. Lowry bored and stroked the engine up to 1900cc and 175 horsepower (!) with Weber carbs, Okrasa heads, Forgedtrue pistons, Sig Erson cam, snaking Empi exhaust, and mated it to a Porsche transmission. With smoking tires on the starting line and lifted front wheels on the 1-2 shift, the Empi VW proved so strong against existing records that NHRA rules were consequently changed to give an I/G class to those who could not compete with the Beetle.

Six-cylinder standouts over the years are an equally compelling incentive for more budget-type gassers. Jerry Haley, Becker-O'Connell, and Loran Sapp took different approaches to F and G/G success, but all made the grade at national races.

Haley hustled an uncommon six-carb GMC/'33 Plymouth around Midwest strips during the early '60s, going two full years with only two defeats. His F/G six cut 13.80/102.24 numbers for '61–'62 Nationals class victory, and looked for all the world like an A/Gasser. The body was virtually stock with only minor changes such as replacement of the headlights with miniature units from a Ford tractor, and use of nerf bars in place of bumpers. The interior was stripped, but clean, complete with bucket seats from a Packard hearse. The drive train was late-model Chevy with three-speed transmission and eight-inch slicks.

Flathead Ford fans found a champion in Bing's Speed Shop at the same time. California shop operator Ed Binggeli built up a '41 Willys F/G winner with care, and it paid off in records as tough as 12.55/107. A major factor in Bing's success was his ability to cut the weight to 2100 pounds, which he accomplished by using a tube front axle assembly, gutting the interior, and re-

Top: The success of "High & Mighty" team in A and B/SR has been achieved with late-model hemi Dodge engine and Torque Flite transmission a la Super Stock. Ohio entries stay at the top of these classes with records and major wins in immaculate pickups.

Bottom: The Anglia body became "the only way to go" for small engine gas coupes during the mid-60s. Light, and on 90-inch wheelbase, the coupes were—and still are—winners, with injected Chevy power. Ed Payne and the Kohler Bros. prove it before a crowd of forty thousand at the National Championships.

placing the seats with VW units. His 286-inch "flattie" was not radical, but it was more than sufficient with three Strombergs. The drive train was traditional '39 Ford transmission coupled to a Halibrand quick-change rear. The result was record-setting enjoyment for $1200.

Dick Becker and John O'Connell employed a '50 Anglia two-door and 320-cubic-inch GMC six for a first-class package and 12.20/113 bursts by 1965. The Sunland, California, pair spent $3500 to build it. Hand-fashioned suspension and carefully engineered and constructed frame were responsible for some of its reputation; twin AFB carbs, four-speed transmission and big slicks, the remainder.

An even stronger "G," owned and driven by long-time Hudson stalwart Loran Sapp, entered later to shake V8 lovers with 11.92/115 mph strength. The "Little Toad's" impressive record resulted from a lot of work by its owner, who fashioned the fuel injection, head modifications, and other parts because no speed equipment units were made. Extensive suspension building complemented a stick-hydro and Mercury rear end.

The 1968 rules brought on a merger of blown modified sports and street roadsters into gas coupe classes as part of an effort to keep meet entries high enough to guarantee spirited competition. The blown gassers had to keep on their toes lest a "furriner" steal their thunder. But, in general, the bracket remained at the status quo — a lot of action for the money whether powered by a "six" or a blown Chrysler.

The Sanitary Qualifiers Car Club entry in '68 Winternationals was one of very few D/G cars with a pre-1955 birthdate. Chevys of '55-'57 dominate the class, but the Ford coupe made a fine showing as a club project.

6

Street Roadsters

The gas coupe's topless counterpart in drag racing, the Street Roadster, is the truest classic of hot rods in the game, but it is hard pressed to remain a major element in the rapidly changing world of the quarter-mile.

Confronted with radical new rules and cars that are faster, more streamlined, and exciting in appearance, and which appeal to the young generation of spectators (who have little appreciation of '32 Fords), street roadsters have declined in numbers and popularity. The latest setback suffered by the old-timers was a 1968 reclassification (due to limited entry) which erased their longstanding identity by moving them into the gas supercharged designation (AA-CC/GS).

Only the roadsters with blowers were so affected, but they had most of the diminishing glamor and appeal remaining in the division. Three classes of prewar bodies with nothing stronger than injected engines were left to fight for a place in the contemporary drag racing picture. A, B, and C/Street Roadsters make up a very small percentage of any meet's entry total, and a mere half-dozen persevering drivers rule the frequently overlooked bracket. This situation could well lead to complete extinction of these drag racing pioneers, an inevitable step as the sport develops into a spectator giant, perhaps, but a sacrilege for those that have held the street roadsters in reverence.

Other roadsters, however, including altered and modified versions, have maintained their appeal to racers and crowds with developments in speed and appearance as evidenced in the 200-mph blown fuel Chrysler altereds. The roadster style will not fade entirely from the scene.

The street roadster is, of course, the oldest vestige of the dry lakes and very first drag strip races. Light and streamlined in comparison to many sedans, roadsters were a first choice for most of drag racing's predecessors, and were converted from lake bed top-speed use to acceleration sprints when the latter caught on in 1948. Ingenious racers had already discovered the performance value of channeling the body (lowering the body on the frame), removing fenders and windshield, and their machines were clearly the ancestors of modern altered and modified roadsters.

Hot but street-legal soft-tops doubled as drive-in terrors and drag strip machines for the majority of rodders that wanted more from their wheels than an occasional race outing. They thrived in California where speed equipment was born and where the weather permitted convertible transportation year 'round. Filled with full-house flatheads, and subsequently with hefty ohv V8 power when the Cad and Olds were released, the early street roadsters were like gas coupes with style.

Their number was made up of racers who could have entered as altereds with cut-down bodies and nitro in the tank (as many did to gain a few miles an hour), but who chose racing's street section as the ideal test of what could be done with ingenuity within a set of strictly confining rules. Altereds and modifieds were allowed engine relocation, inside gutting, removal of body parts, and other major reconstruction, whereas street roadsters were held to engine modification and very little else. Running the SR's was therefore more of a challenge to driver skill and preparation, for the cars were closely matched — as opposed to their wide-open brothers.

STARS-TO-BE IN STREET ROADSTERS

Don Nicholson was one of these fendered fighters 'way back in 1953, before he became "Dyno Don" in Super Stocks, and long before he became the sport's most famous funny car driver. The Pasadena Chevy lover captured A/SR class at NHRA's Pacific Southwest Championships at Paradise Mesa Drag Strip, proving street machine talent that would later earn him many national titles.

Carl Stone was another one who leveled the competition, with his notorious "Rolling Stone" A/SR from Texas. His was a popular combination of the period: flathead engine and '32 Ford body, capable of knocking off the bigger ohv-powered cars. Stone remained a top roadster threat from a 1954 Southwest Regional A/SR upset of Jim Govro's Cad-powered machine at 14.51/96.05, to a 1957 Nationals B/SR class win of 13.97/98.03 for which a new Chevy engine replaced the flathead.

A Boise, Idaho, driver who came to be one of the ranking gas dragster racers, Harrell Amyx, was also in street roadsters at the time. His Buick/'27 "T" hit 85.55 in topping the B/SR class at the 1955 Northwest Safari stop. Amyx moved to Los Angeles and later became a central figure in national drag racing safety legislation until he died at the wheel in May 1966. His powerful blown Chrysler AA/GD, one of the first to break eight-second e.t.'s, in keeping with a trend by gas dragsters to achieve extreme light weight, was not equipped with a crankshaft support or a strap around the roll bar. Both items were made mandatory by sanctioning organizations after Amyx's engine exploded and the crank dropped out of the car, causing him to crash at speed. The possibility that he sustained fatal injuries when his helmet protruded between the roll bar struts and was then unprotected prompted a ruling on roll bar straps.

Otie Smith, the Akron, Ohio, speed shop operator whose wild blown fuel altereds drew raves in the '60's, was opening the door in 1956 with a big B/SR win. His Chevy-powered 14.23/95.03 clocking took the New York Regional trophy.

The first chance to attain a National Cham-

pionship win was provided in 1955 by the big
Great Bend, Kansas, event. Roadsters from all over
the country met, and Owen Bowling of San Gabriel, California, took top honors at 111.11 mph
in his '52 Chrysler/'29 Ford A/SR. Also notable
as a C/SR winner was Dale Ham, now an NHRA
Division Director. His '54 Dodge/'29 Ford from
Amarillo cut 94.24-mph speeds.

Ever-changing rules were soon to abolish the
"C" category, though, and in '56 there were only
two Street Roadster divisions. The classifications
were A/SR from 0 to 8.59 pounds per cubic inch,
and B/SR from 8.60 up. General rules requiring
an American-made roadster body without alteration and with full street equipment remained in-
tact.

Very similar to their hard-top counterparts, the
gas coupes, most competitive street roadsters
boasted Olds, Chrysler, or Chevy engines in '29
or '32 Fords by this time, and racers the country
over hustled them to about 95 mph. The cream
of the crop, which like the gassers were mostly
from Texas, met at the 1957 NHRA Nationals to
turn in the big numbers. A 105.88 in 13.32 seconds won A/SR for Curtis Frank's '57 Chevy/'24
Ford; Stone took "B" at 98.03; and Bill Hopper's
Arizona Chrysler/'29 turned 113.49 mph to become officially fastest of the breed.

SR's underwent little change in the next few
years, as drag racing in general experienced a period of adjustment. The sport was developing into
a big spectator attraction and new Detroit Super
Stock models were topping 100 mph in the quar-

ter. The consequent jockeying around by drivers and strip operators left the street roadsters unscathed.

One of the first prominent thrusts into the limelight by a street roadster was Courtney Scott's 1960 rise to Street Eliminator at the Nationals. The Washington, D.C., B/SR entry motored past winners of all the other street section classes for the crown. Johnny Loper's tough B/Gasser was the last challenger for Scott's '55 DeSoto/'34 Ford, one whom he narrowly nipped in 13.14/108.56.

MOST FAMOUS ROADSTER OF ALL TIME

While Scott, and street roadsters in general, basked in this new recognition, a Ventura, California, project took shape that would rule the bracket until the present day. Hugh Tucker, an experimental machinist, was combining a six-carb 480-inch GMC engine, '34 Ford frame, and '28 Chevy body into the single best street roadster ever built.

Jim Cassidy's Chrysler-powered A/SR record holder prevailed at the '61 Winternationals, and Henry Mullins' East Coast terror won at the Nationals, spoiling Tucker's initial big meet appearance. But when the 1962 Winternationals and Bakersfield Championships came to his own backyard, Tucker began a bracket domination that has no equal in the history of drag racing.

He had improved his "family project" mount since the previous experience and it stood with 475 inches of blown Oldsmobile in a much-im-

proved chassis for the '62 season. The effect was
not only A/SR supremacy at the meets, but the
NHRA Little Eliminator title as well in 11.08/
127.29. He stepped up the pace to 132.35 mph in
topping A/SR at the Nationals, then returned to
the West Coast to prepare for a big '63 showing.

Ironically, Tucker's unique charger was brought
to battle infrequently, entered only in NHRA's
two biggest meets each year, and a few more in
California. Employment demands and economic
practicality imposed such a limited race schedule,
but it proved an effective long range plan, for
Tucker could concentrate on the major races for
maximum results.

The king of the roadsters made a lot of resource-
ful improvements on the high-riding Ventura Motors machine. The blown Olds' torque was controlled by homemade quarter-elliptic rear springs
and a set of real heavyweight traction bars that
weighed eight pounds each despite aluminum
construction. A Watts link was bolted to the differential and frame sides to limit side movement
and improve lateral stability.

Front end construction included a chrome-moly
tube axle with transverse Ford spring, '40 Willys
spindles, and disc brakes, which made it possible
to make adjustments that would exactly meet the
24-inch crankshaft height rule that applies to
street roadsters as well as to gas coupes. Homemade friction shocks and radius rods, and steering
gear pirated from a '59 Ford truck were examples
of Tucker's handiwork.

Specialties on the '28 Chevrolet body included

Top: Car club racing projects are often more fun and less expensive than going it alone. The Pharaoh's Pacers of Southern California found a sponsor in Dick Allen Rambler, and they race their small V8 AMC hardtop with confidence and fun. *Bottom:* This amazing shot of finish line drama at *Hot Rod* magazine meet reveals Hugh Tucker gaining in left lane with faster AA/SR and observing Marrs Boys gasser as they approach the win lights. Race was a near dead-heat, but was spoiled when both broke out of their time brackets by going too fast to beat the other!

aluminum Triumph cycle front fenders; an aluminum hood by Wayne Ewing; miniature Willys radiator; front-mounted Moon fuel tank; '32 grille shell; heavy woodwork in the trunk body; and a huge battery positioned over the right rear wheel. His mother stitched up Naugahyde upholstery; his father handled the bodywork.

The '62 Olds engine was bored, and stroked $\frac{5}{8}$", carried a 6–71 blower, Hilborn upright injectors, and homemade tuned exhaust headers that dumped into an echoing collector on each side.

Drive line and running gear included B & M Hydro-Stick transmission, shortened Pontiac drive shaft, '57 Pontiac rear end with 4.30 to 1 gears. Mag wheels, Buick aluminum rear brakes, Pirelli and 10.00 x 16 M & H tires carried Tucker to victory.

His was not the only roadster that performed notably in '62 — a handful of other record holders were leading the three SR classes. It is interesting that two of these racers, and others to follow, were from Northwest states — a sort of street roadster specialization in that lightly populated region.

Conaway & Woodhouse, a Cheyenne, Wyoming, A/SR team uncorked an official 11.05 with Chevy power, and Portland's Johnny Hart topped the revived flathead class at 13.29/102.38. The best B/SR time, 11.77 seconds, was by Californian Dean Lowe's Chevy.

Rules were revised somewhat for 1963 Street Roadster competition, and a new AA/SR designation was given blown models of 5.00 pounds per cubic inch or less. A/SR was adjusted to 5.00 to 8.59 unblown, "B" became 8.60 and over, "C" remained the range for flathead, six-cylinder, and straight eight engine entries.

More liberal construction rules permitted fiberglass bodies, and — due to a shortage of original roadster bodies — coupe and sedan bodies with tops neatly removed became eligible. Bodies could be channeled a maximum of six inches for streamlining. Windshields were optional equipment, but four street-legal fenders were still required.

Tucker opened the year with a Winternationals AA/SR and Junior Eliminator parlay in 10.30/138.24, smashing the class records, and he repeated at Bakersfield. Charlie Smith topped winter A/SRs in his Chevy-powered Oklahoma City national record holder that he drove to 11.12/125.88 before giving in to temptation and switching to the faster altered bracket. His decision proved fortuitous — Smith became 1964 World Competition Eliminator in the A/A.

The eastern team of Reider-Weiler became the bracket's big item later in the year, charging to the '63 Nationals Junior Eliminator win after besting B/SR. Tucker nearly gave the roadsters a double, but a freak situation gave George Montgomery's A/GS the Middle Eliminator payoff. The trusty AA/SR suffered a battery failure in the staging lanes and was unable to start for the big run!

A new trend in street roadsters was brought to the Nationals in the form of Jim Parsons' A/SR.

The Ohio entry featured a '63 Dodge Ramcharger engine and TorqueFlite transmission — the power train of a MoPar Super Stock. This combination proved so reliable, and fit the class requirements so well, that Parsons and similar "As" continued to lead the class as late as 1968.

Olds power was not easily overcome, however. Hugh Tucker and Jerry Hays swept the top two classes at the '64 Winternationals. Tucker rang up the first major meet nine-second street roadster time, a sensational 9.91/147.73 in winning AA/SR, a feat he nearly duplicated a month later with a Bakersfield 9.97/147. Hays' immaculate Olds "Street Cleaner" emerged from "A."

Most interesting records of the year were the AHRA 11.57 mark established in A/SR by Ed Martin's 427 Ford/'32 from Indianapolis, and another Northwest standard, this one by Clarence Everett's flathead C/SR.

THE FIELD NARROWS

Two dozen top competitors controlled Street Roadster activities through the next few years as entry totals diminished in the face of faster and more contemporary cars. There was very little technical development in the street roadsters, unlike the gas coupes and altereds, but there were at least two fine performances during 1965. Tucker, still on top, strolled 10.03 for Winternationals AA/SR and Super Eliminator titles. Joe Cunningham, a colorful 300-pounder from Wichita, Kansas, became a national figure after sweeping

the $3000 Springnationals Street Eliminator field
with his Chevy Six C/SR.

Lawlis and Remmy made another Super Stock
Dodge A/SR pay in a Nationals class win of
10.38/133.33, continuing the S/S takeover which
was carried on by Parsons in 10.16/138.46 the following year, and by both in 1967. They split official A/SR records of 140.84 mph and 9.95 seconds.

Taking a cue from gas coupe leaders "Big John"
Mazmanian and Stone-Woods-Cook, who went to
blown Chrysler engines after their Olds became
inadequate for ever-bigger numbers, Hugh Tucker
picked up a hemi of his own and opened new
horizons for his silver veteran.

The '66 Pomona meet Super Eliminator bracket
fell to the new power, and the Chrysler enabled a
great 9.75 e.t. at only 125 mph as Tucker also took
Nationals AA/SR. The hemi, now entered from
Van Nuys, also came within one final heat with
the Kohler Brothers of repeating its Super win
the following winter.

Tucker's future under the new rules, i.e., as a
AA/GS, with the gassers and modified sports, was
uncertain because subtle rules differences kept
roadster performance slightly behind comparably
classed gassers. Wheelbase length has been one of
the distinctions. Although the ruled minimum for
both gas coupes and roadsters had been 92 inches
until 1968 (then 90 inches), the rule applicable to
both specifically reads, ". . . must retain stock
wheelbase and tread width for car body used."
Street roadsters, however, are limited to American-

made bodies, and gas coupes are not, so the British Anglias, Austins, and Prefects that smart gassers now use are outside street roadster legality. Their short wheelbase advantage is clear in observing A/GS progress after reaching 9.80-second elapsed times by 102-inch Willys.

John Mazmanian built a new short Austin that almost immediately leaped to 8.90-second times, with the same Chrysler engine from the nine-second era, but there are no American bodies that would allow street roadsters much reduction from Tucker's 104-inch length, and his e.t.'s have been on the same 9.80 plane since 1964.

Year-end 1967 national records of the three types, for instance, were: AA/G — 8.93/162.12; AA/MSP — 9.23/155.44; AA/SR — 9.79/148.27. Most of Tucker's roadster success was based on the fact it was the strongest around, and Tucker could thus set the class record at will and then run very close to it in NHRA's Eliminator handicap system. Under 1968 classification this was not possible, and even the few fine AA/SR's remaining may be slowly phased out.

BIG "LITTLE GUYS"

Outstanding unblown street roadsters since 1966 have taken more than their share of major wins, and are led, ironically, by the slowest class of all. Joe Cunningham and Jan Riedel pushed C/SR class records to amazing 10.90/122.51 levels with Chevy sixes and became important considerations every time the Street Eliminator field ap-

This sanitary B & W Transmission Special from South Gate, California is about as big as street roadsters go. Complete with grille shell, fenders, and other class requirements, the massive blown Chrysler engine carries it to 140 mph speeds.

proached the line. Riedel finished the '67 season as runner-up to the World Street Champion.

Racing "C's," or other street roadsters for that matter, on a budget is becoming increasingly attractive as entries remain low in number while the opposing brackets expand. There is enough competition within the classes to keep them challenging, but in the event they are depleted in any particular region the Street Eliminator workout against other class winners is certain to take up the slack. Many present and prospective SR drivers actually look on their elite status as a blessing, because an entry into the lucrative Eliminator bracket from a class with only two or three cars is like money in the bank. There's no prize money for class wins, and many people feel that drag racing should not be a hard-fought class win over twenty-five challengers, but a handicap win over a trio of other class victors that pays off handsomely.

Top: The Cabriolets (NHA Charter) Road Club of Hialeah, Florida exhibits a fine array of machinery and a comfortable clubhouse. Quantity speed equipment discounts, tips from other members on improving e.t.s, "loans" from the club funds, and a convenient place to work on the cars are the advantages of an active club.

Bottom: Driving a beautiful street rod like this is a thrill usually possible only through car club membership.

7

Car Clubs and Fun

The amazing growth of drag racing has had at least one ill effect. Car clubs, which were responsible for much of the initial growth, diminished in popularity as racing expanded in the 1960's. However, revival efforts enacted simultaneously by Detroit automakers and the National Hot Rod Association have injected new interest and enthusiasm into the club activity since 1965.

Car clubs were very important as far back as the 1930's, since they were the only link among the many street racers who cruised Los Angeles, the birthplace of hot rods. The small nucleus from which drag racing evolved had only word-of-mouth communication, and relied on informal "club" gatherings to get word around of any pending river bed face-off, parties, or parts for sale.

The Knight Riders hot rod club, the Road Runners, Throttlers, Sidewinders, Bungholers, Desert Goats, Rattlers, Revs, and dozens of others were gathering at Scully's Cafe, in garages, and in club rooms to plan their next assault on the dry lakes and to discuss the problem of increased attention by police. Eventually they all met to schedule a

1938 interclub race, and called the larger organization the Southern California Timing Association. Rival groups formed the Western, Rusetta, Bell, and Mojave Timing Associations.

Rodders had a little more support from civic officials after they organized, but as their club names indicate, not all were dedicated to cooperation with the law. For them, public acceptance was hard to obtain, so there was another attraction among this misunderstood element: Clubs were a sort of fraternity, providing the only opportunity for rodders to enjoy their enthusiasm for speed while they were in town. Civic projects and sponsorship by community businesses were to come much later.

World War II interrupted the racers' plans, but after the war an enormous number of young drivers and their modified cars flooded Southern California. A half-dozen drive-ins served as informal meeting places before an evening's street races. The situation became intolerable to Los Angeles police and they responded by "pinching" anything that even looked like a hot rod, whether it was moving or not. In order to cool the situation, the drivers formed organized clubs with rules and penalties about street racing. Soon afterward, the Pomona, California, Choppers and the Autocrats from Redlands staged one of the very first drag races (1949) at the Fontana Airport with assistance from Chief Ralph Parker and officer Bud Coons of the Pomona Police Department.

The Memphis, Tennessee, Rodders were laying plans for drag races in the same year. The Cam

Jammers of Akron, Ohio; the Caddo Mills, Texas, Chapparals; and the Denver Timing Association opened events shortly thereafter.

Club effort was usually the only means by which a drag strip could be found in local communities, and NHRA's Safety Safaris of 1954–1956 gave hundreds of clubs from coast to coast chances to impress local officials with the sales pitches of the traveling drag racing salesmen of the Safari.

CLUBS ON THEIR WAY OUT — THEN IN

This encouraged support, and by the late 1950's, some 150 drag strips resulted. Although the Smokers introduced the initial Bakersfield Fuel and Gas Championship in 1959, club interest began to taper off with the entrance of professional dragstrip promoters and the dilution of the "hardcore" modified early model hot rodder ranks at the races by a new breed — the drivers of stock cars who were not hot rodders and didn't want the name. Stockers were faster than many classic rods by 1961, and the whole club system began to seem irrelevant since the rods on which they had been founded were no longer "in." The clubs dwindled.

Later, as manufacturers realized the sales and public relations value of such promotion, they began to sponsor clubs made up almost entirely of stockers. Races, rallies, and tech sessions at the dealers' were the attractions of Mustang, Barracuda, and Javelin clubs. Corvette clubs had been active for years, though they did not generally emphasize drag racing. The 1966 formation of an NHRA Charter Club program further rejuvenated the club idea.

Clubs provide good fellowship, exchange of ideas and information, and project participation such as drag racing that is not possible on an individual basis. But proper formation and organization are essential to take advantage of these benefits.

HOW TO FORM A SUCCESSFUL CLUB

Only a small number of interested persons is required — often less than a dozen — to form a club. Establish a planning group to set down purposes and goals, and prepare a proposed constitution with by-laws for presentation to the members at the first general meeting.

Conduct meetings by parliamentary procedure in order to attain maximum results and enjoyment, keeping the meeting's business and tedium brief. Appoint a temporary group of officers to conduct business until the constitution is accepted, then install permanent officers chosen by election. Select a straightforward name that has no double meaning, or "outlaw" connotation and is not offensive.

Sponsorship of a local business or civic group is not easy to arrange at first, but it can generally provide the club with a meeting place where records and equipment can be maintained. A sponsor's good reputation can also serve to gain the cooperation of others for activities and projects when the time comes. In this area of soliciting community cooperation, a well-respected advisor can also be of great assistance as a liaison between club and community.

The many potential sponsor groups interested in youth and highway safety include: safety councils, service clubs, churches, chambers of commerce, auto clubs, police departments, auto dealers, radio-TV stations, newspapers, and schools.

The success of any club depends largely on the activities it undertakes. The more variety offered through a well-planned program, the better chance a club has of keeping its members' interest. A diversified schedule also serves to gain the recognition and public understanding that every bona fide club seeks, as well as a healthy club treasury.

Some of the very active clubs of today are the New Breed Drag Team of Norwich, Connecticut; Bonanza Rambler Club, North Hollywood, California; South Bay Racing Association, Manhattan Beach, California; the Coachmen, South Bend, Indiana; Low Risers Club, Dearborn, Michigan; and of course the racing Ramchargers of Detroit. They keep club interest at a peak by staging regular races and special projects that suit each club. Some of these projects are outlined below as examples of proven fun activities for members and friends.

ACTIVITIES MAKE IT FUN

DRIVING SKILL CONTESTS. These events require only the proper area, such as a large, empty parking lot, rubber pylons, and measuring equipment. Various popular patterns of forward and backward maneuvering include the Irish Reel, Texas Star, Scorpion, Garage Parking, Limited Area Turn, the time-proven Slalom, and Parallel Parking. Based on a point system, these competitions are open to all, with little danger.

SPECIAL RUNS. The Reliability Run is about the most popular club driving activity, determining the reliability of both car and driver. The host club should select a varied course through the city and establish distance and time between certain "check points." Organize check stations to be manned by several members to record the arrival of each contestant.

Draw up a course map with speed averages for prerace presentation to entrants. Mark each car's number on the side which will face the check stations for easy identification.

The drivers are to cover each leg of the course in as close to the prescribed time as possible. Points are scored against drivers for arriving at stations too early as well as too late — one point per minute as computed by the check stations. A celebration dinner is the most popular way to close a club Reliability Run.

Variations include a Scrambled Egg Run in which course instructions are garbled, and a Secret Time Run in which the leg times are not announced until after the run.

The Economy Run is a contest to determine who can drive the greatest number of miles on a premeasured amount of gasoline. Poker Runs are won by the contestant who finds hidden playing cards on a driving course that make up the best poker hand.

Highway Bingo, using a puzzling "key" chart and a check point time schedule, and the Quiz Run, in which speed is not all-important (the kind girl friends can join), are equal fun. True and false questions lead to segmented clues that contestants find and follow to the end of the Quiz Run.

The Map Run employs a carefully measured map drawn on a blank paper with only mileage numbers and the North direction in addition to a direction line. Drivers follow their speedometers to achieve a correct course, try for the lowest elapsed time.

A unique Slick Stop Run is staged on a purposely slippery surface, rewarding the shortest stopping distance on icy or wet pavement. Permission from law enforcement agencies to use a block long stretch of paved street and guards to supervise the traffic are required, as are a fire hose during warm weather, sawhorses, and rubber highway pylons.

Each driver must approach the collapsible target pylon on three attempts (from 10, 20, and 30 mph), brake to a four-wheel slide, and stop within one foot of the pylon without striking it. Points are deducted at the rate of one point for each foot distance from the pylon to the car when it stops.

CIVIC PROGRAMS. Progressive car clubs find community projects profitable in terms of actual cash, public acceptance, and new friends. They negotiate with various civic groups to provide the manpower and services for their upcoming project(s), then pitch in, although the activities are most often not auto oriented.

The March of Dimes, Heart Fund, Tuberculosis Society, Red Cross, Salvation Army, and other organizations conduct annual fund-raising drives for which they need collection and office help.

Civil Defense and other emergency services frequently need a supply of cars and drivers in case of flood, fire, etc.

Christmas-present programs in conjunction with a civic group or independently as a club are rewarding to orphanages and hospitals, but even more so to the giving club.

FUND-RAISING AND OTHER SPECIAL PROJECTS. The Club Car Wash is the most profitable activity for most clubs. The club reserves the wash stalls of a local service station, or sets up a wash station in a large parking lot for a Saturday or Sunday of rubbing and scrubbing.

The preparation of posters and other advertising measures should keep from ten to twenty-five club members busy all day, each with his own assignment. A one-dollar charge in most areas will be less than that of the "competition," yet sufficient to show a tidy profit.

Club Auctions are among the most interesting participation activities. A collection of miscellaneous automotive, garage, and other parts and pieces donated by members will usually attract a crowd ranging from housewives to junk dealers for a day of bidding.

Sponsorship of social gatherings such as dances will introduce the club to many new friends and provide still another boost for the treasury.

Public Relations efforts by clubs can be inexpensive if members will offer their showy cars to State and County Fairs, gala parades, or for a club-sponsored car show. A Good Neighbor Weekend in which the club provides the community with free twenty-four-hour road service for a weekend will also win civic support. Appointment of a committee to gather battery, tire, and other equipment necessary for such an emergency operation should precede an active publicity campaign to make the good work known.

Another valuable club service to render is participation in Safe Driver Week. Coordination with the local police or highway patrol will make this an "official" undertaking worthy of considerable notice by the press. During this week, club members dispense Safe Driver cards to a small number of citizens they observe doing a proper job behind the wheel, and the recipients gather later for a written examination. The overall winner is proclaimed Mr. Safe Driver of the city.

There are, at present, hundreds of active clubs, most sharing drag racing as a basic interest. Each has its own slate of other activities, but they all have one thing in common — fun with their cars.

Write to NHRA Charter Clubs, 3418 West First Street, Los Angeles, California 90004 for many other interesting ideas for clubs and their activities.

Glossary

"A" or A-Bone — Model "A" Ford.

Alky — Alcohol; used as a racing fuel and usually mixed with nitromethane.

Altered — A competition class requiring the use of an automobile body, but permitting extensive modifications. Generally the cars in this class run without fenders or glass. Drivers may be moved to the rear, as are the engines, for better weight distribution.

Anchors — Brakes.

Asphalt eater — A top-performing dragster.

Ballast — Weight added to a car to bring it up to legal poundage.

Bang shift hydro — A hydromatic transmission that can be held in any gear for racing.

Banzai — An all-out run.

Bench racing — Talking a good race.

Bent eight — V8 engine.

Bent stovebolt — Chevrolet V8 engine.

Big arm — A long piston stroke.

Big end — The end of the quarter-mile racing distance. It is here that the cars reach their highest speeds and where the supercharged engines have a definite advantage.

Big rumper — A big, bad engine.

Big wienie — A top driver.

Binders — Brakes.

Bite — Traction.

Blacky carbon — Gasoline; term is usually used by racers who burn the exotic fuel mixtures permitted in the unlimited dragster classes.

Blinkey — The timing light at the finish line.

Blow — An engine failure.

Blower — A supercharger; also known as a *huffer, pump, stuffer,* or *windmill.*

Blown — Supercharged.

Blown engine — An engine using a supercharger.

Blown gasser — A supercharged, gas-burning engine.

Bobbed — Cut or shortened; the term is usually applied to fenders.

Boost — The manifold pressure supplied by a supercharger.

Boots — Tires.

Bore — The diameter of the cylinder.

"Bored and stroked" — The cylinder bore and the length of the piston stroke have been increased.

Bottom end — The part of the engine that includes the crankshaft, main bearings, and connecting rod bearings.

Box — The transmission.

Brain Bucket — A safety helmet.

Broke — Out of competition due to mechanical failure.

Bucket seat — A contour-shaped seat.

"Bucks up" — "In the money."

Bug catcher — The scoop or hood around the injector system on a supercharged engine.

Bumblebee — A small, foreign car.

Bump stick — The engine camshaft. (The term comes from the lobes on the cam.)

Buttons — Chrysler Corporation stock cars equipped with pushbutton-operated automatic transmissions.

Bye — A single run made during eliminations to equalize the number of runs made by each contestant. Bye runs are made when an uneven number of cars advance to the next round of competition.

Cam — The camshaft.

Can — Nitromethane racing fuel.

Carb — The carburetor.

Carolina stocker, Southern stocker — A stock car running with illegal engine size or equipment.

Carry the wheels — To pick up front wheels when coming off the line.

Channeled — Having body floor repositioned in order to lower overall height.

Cheater slicks — Special tires made of racing-rubber compounds, but with tread design simulating regular street tires.

Chevy — Chevrolet engine.

Chizler — Chrysler engine.

Chopped — Cut down in size, such as when a portion of body top is removed for lowering, or with material removed from flywheel.

Christmas tree — An electronic countdown starter;

a set of varied, colored lights on a short pole, used to start races. Its major feature is its ability to handicap the faster car running against a slower class opponent.

Chromies — Simulated magnesium racing wheels or chromed wheels used to dress up a car.

Chrondeks — The electronic timing system used at most drag racing events.

Chute — The parachute used to stop a high-speed race car at the end of the drag strip.

Clutch-off — To raise the clutch and accelerate rapidly, as in the start of a drag race.

Cool Can — A device consisting of a canister filled with ice in which a portion of the fuel line (between the fuel pump and the carburetor) is coiled. This lowers the temperature of the gasoline for improved performance.

Coughed engine — An engine that has really failed.

Crank — The crankshaft.

Cubes — Cubic inches of displacement in an engine.

Cut — To eliminate another car from race.

Cut a fat one — To run at top speed.

Dohc — Double overhead camshaft.

Dagoed — Having a dropped front axle.

Daylighting — Being so far ahead of another car that there is daylight between them.

Deuce — A 1932 Ford; one of the true pioneers of the hot-rod movement.

Dial-a-Winner — The Dodge push-button automatic transmission.

Dog clutch — The in-out type clutch that uses a gear shift to couple the engine to the drive shaft.

Drag — Quarter-mile acceleration race between two cars.

Drag strip — A strip of pavement 60 feet wide and 4000 feet long used for drag racing.

Draggin-wagon — A truck used for drag racing; sometimes, a really fast racing car.

Dragster — A specially designed race car for quarter-mile acceleration events. The most popular design locates the driver behind the rear wheels for maximum traction.

Draw — Method of determining opponents and lanes prior to competition, especially among Top Fuel and Top Gas dragsters.

D-ring — The ring or handle the driver pulls at the end of the run to open the safety chute.

Drop the hammer — To rapidly engage the clutch at the start of a race.

Elapsed time — The number of seconds and fractions of a second required to cover the 1320-foot racing distance. The millisecond electronic timers start when the car leaves the starting line and stop when it crosses the finish line at the end of the quarter-mile. The speed clocks are located 66 feet on either side of the quarter-mile finish line, forming a 132-foot-trap.

Eliminated — Beaten in a race.

Exotic fuel — Alcohols, nitromethane, and other fuels besides gasoline.

Eyes — The light beams that stop and start the electronic timers on the strip.

Factory experimental — A limited production stock car.

Filled — A car is said to be filled when the gaps in welded body panel joints have been concealed.

Filled axle — A dropped front axle with portions of "I" beam section filled with metal for added strength.

Fire suit — Aluminized fireproof driver's uniform worn by drag racers in all fuel-burning cars; also called flame suit.

Flagman — The official who starts the race at tracks not equipped with electronic starting system.

Flat out — Driving at top speed.

Flathead — An early model Ford engine with valves located in the block; an L-head or side valve engine.

Flexi-flyer — A long wheelbase dragster with built-in flexibility which helps keep wheels on strip.

Flyboy — A weekend-only drag racer.

FoMoCo — Ford Motor Company.

Forked-eight — V8 engine.

Foul — To leave the starting line before the green light. This action causes a red light to flash.

Four-on-the-floor — A manually operated four-speed transmission.

Four-banger — A four-cylinder engine, usually an early model Ford or Chevrolet.

Fuelie, fueler, or fuel burner — A car that burns special racing fuels rather than gasoline.

Full bore — With throttle wide open.

Full house — A highly modified racing engine.

Funny car — An altered wheelbase competition

car just barely resembling a stock car.

FX car — A factory experimental class car.

Gasser — A racing car that burns gas, competing in either Gas Coupe/Sedan (G) or Supercharged Gas Coupe/Sedan (GS) class. The latter is called a blown gasser.

Gearbox — The transmission.

Genuine racer — A confirmed drag racer.

Getting out of it — Lifting one's foot from the accelerator.

Glass — Fiberglass components for an automobile, such as fenders, hoods, and doors. They are used to minimize weight on a race car.

Glass-wrapped — Having a chassis with a fiberglass body.

Gold — Trophies.

Goodies — Extra engine equipment.

Gourd guard — Crash helmet.

Grind — The cam lobe contour, i.e., street grind, full-race grind, etc.

Gutted — Having all interior removed, including excess instruments and equipment.

Handler — Driver.

Hang a left, (or) right — To turn left or right.

Hat — Crash helmet.

Hauler — An exceptionally fast car.

Haulin' Henry — A fast Ford.

Hauling the mail — Running at top speed.

Headers — Free-flow exhaust manifolds that permit smooth, uninterrupted expulsion of the burned gasses from the engine.

Hemi — An engine equipped with hemispherical combustion chamber heads.

Henry — A Ford Motor Company product.

Highboy — A coupe, sedan, or roadster whose body is on top of frame rails at stock height.

Hole shot — To beat opponent away from starting line; e.g., "He put a 20-foot hole shot on him."

Honker — An exceptionally fast or quick car, generally, a stock car.

Horse car — Ford Mustang.

Hose brakes — Hydraulic brakes.

Hot dog, hot shoe, etc. — A top driver.

Huffer — A supercharger.

Hydro — Automatic transmission.

Igniter — Ignition distributor.

In the chute — Positioned in the staging area, ready to race.

Injected — Equipped with a fuel injection system.

Injector — Fuel injection system. Metering units that feed gasoline or fuel directly into the engine, replacing the more conventional carburetors and greatly improving the power and efficiency of the engine.

Jimmy — A GMC truck engine, modified for racing.

Joe logbolt — A driver who races only on weekends.

Jug — Carburetor.

Juice — Nitromethane and other special racing fuel additives.

Juice brakes — Hydraulic brakes.

Jump — To leave the starting line ahead of the green light. This is a foul and the driver is eliminated.

Knock-off — A quickly removable wheel lug.

Kooky — A bobtail roadster.

Lay rubber — To spin wheels on the pavement.

Lead sled — A slow car; one with poor acceleration.

Light the rugs, light the tires — To accelerate so that tires smoke.

Lights — The lights that start the electronic timing system at the beginning of a run and stop the clocks at the completion of a run.

Locked rear end — Having a rear axle with gears modified to eliminate differential action.

Loose track — A wet dragstrip.

Lose the fire — To stall the engine.

Loser's leave — A starting system with a single amber light and random time lapse before "go" light flashes.

Loud pedal — Gas pedal.

Low end — The low engine speed range where torque is usually best.

Lunch at engine — To scatter parts around the track during extreme engine failure.

Mag — A magneto.

Mags — Custom made magnesium wheels; now, also any wheel resembling a magnesium wheel.

Mains — Main bearings.

Match race — A two-out-of-three or three-out-of-five race between cars.

Mean motor scooter — A hot-running engine.

Midnight auto parts — Parts stolen from other cars.

Mill — Engine.

Molded — Having body contours and panel joints worked into continuous smooth surface.

MoPar — Chrysler Corporation product.

Nitro — Nitromethane; a special racing fuel which produces much higher horsepower ratings than automobile pump gasoline.

Oasis — Refreshment stand.

Off the line, Out of the chute, Out of the gate, Out of the hole — Start of race.

Ohc — Overhead camshaft.

Ohv — Overhead valves.

On the wood — Running at full throttle.

Over-bore — Larger than stock cylinder diameter.

Peak out — To rev the engine to its limit.

Peaked — Having on ornamental raised bead worked into metal.

Percentage — Mixture of nitromethane and alcohol used in race cars. A car on 80 percent would be burning 80 percent nitro and 20 percent alcohol.

"Plant it" — Run at full throttle.

Poncho — A hot Pontiac.

Pop — Nitromethane fuel additive.

Pop the clutch — To engage the clutch suddenly.

Ported — An engine is said to have been ported when its intake and exhaust passages have been enlarged to improve engine breathing.

Pot — Carburetor.

Puffer, Pump — Supercharger.

Pump stuff — Gasoline.

Push car — A regular car used to start a race car that is not equipped with a starter. All necessary spare parts and equipment are also carried in the push car.

Put in the can — To operate the race car on the largest possible percentage of fuel.

Put it to the wood — To open the throttle to its maximum.

Quick-change rear end — A rear axle equipped with gears in center section that may be changed quickly to alter ratios.

Ragtop — Convertible.

Rail — A dragster.

Rail job — A dragster without a body.

Raked — Having one end of the car noticeably lower than the other.

Rat — Badly running car.

Ratchet jaw — A person who talks a great deal without saying much.

Raunchy — Unattractive or dirty.

Relieved — When the intake and exhaust passages have had obstructions removed from them in order to improve engine breathing.

Resin — Liquid or powder put on tires for better traction.

Reverses — Wheels with rims turned around for a wider track.

Roll bar — Hollow steel tubing that forms a protective "cage" around the driver in case of accident.

Roller — A camshaft setup. The camshaft operates in connection with a roller tappet device instead of a direct contact flat tappet.

"Run whatcha brung" — No-holds-barred race with no rules.

Sam Sled — A slow driver.

Sandbagger — A driver who holds back in the staging area to select his opponents during elimination races; a poor sport.

Sauce — Nitromethane and alcohol mixture fuel.

Scattershield, Lower cover — A protective shield around flywheel and clutch.

Seagull — Someone who complains constantly.

Sectioning — Reducing car's height or width by cutting out a section of the body.

Setup — Carburetor(s) and manifold system.

Sewing machine — A small foreign car.

Shaved — Having ornamentation removed from car body.

Shoes — Tires.

Shut down — Beaten.

Shut of — To lift the foot off the accelerator pedal.

Shutdown area — The portion of the dragstrip beyond timing lights.

Six-holder — Six-cylinder engine.

Skins — Tires.

Slicks — Wide, flat, smooth-tread tires providing maximum traction; designed exclusively for use on the rear wheels of drag racing vehicles.

Slingshot — Dragster in which driver sits behind the rear wheels for maximum weight distribution and traction.

Slippery — Streamlined.

Slug — Piston.

Slush pump — Automatic transmission.

Smoke off — To leave the starting line first.

Smoothed — Shaved.

Solids — Solid, mechanical valve lifters.

Solo — An individual run down a drag strip.

Speed shift — To shift gears rapidly without releasing accelerator.

Spokes — Bicyclelike wheels used on front of dragster.

Spook — A car that leaves the starting line too soon.

Stack — A short, individual intake or exhaust pipe.

"Stand on it" — Run at full throttle.

Stick shift — Manual-shift transmission.

Stocker — Stock production automobile.

Stovebolt — A Chevrolet.

Stroke — The distance the piston travels in the cylinder.

"Stroke it" — Take it easy.

Stroker — An engine in which the piston stroke has been increased over the original measurement.

Stuffer — A supercharger.

Swing pedals — The clutch or brake pedals that

are attached to firewall instead of going through the floor.

Tach — Tachometer; a device which shows the engine rpm.

T-bone — A Model T Ford.

Tech — Technical inspection of each race car for safety and classification.

Tipping the gas — Filling the tank.

Top — Top Eliminator (see below).

Top eliminator (T.E.) — The only car remaining in a class after elimination runs.

Top end — A car's highest power output; also, second half of a drag strip run.

Top time — The terminal speed attained by a drag racing vehicle on a run.

Toy — A race car.

Traps — An electronic light system at the finish line which stops the elapsed-time clocks and gives the vehicle's top speed. Also, the timing area itself.

Trick engine, transmission, etc. — Having special components not normally used.

Trophy run — The final run for a class or eliminator victory.

Tube steak — A hot dog; the main staple of a drag racer's meal.

Twilight zone — Speeds in excess of 200 mph.

Typewriter — Dodge push-button automatic transmission.

Unglue — To blow up an engine.

Ventilate the block — To put a rod out through the engine.

'Vette — Corvette.

Wail — To run really fast.

Weekend warrior — A dragster who races only on weekends.

Wheelstand — When rapid acceleration lifts the front end of a race car from the pavement coming off the starting line. Also called a wheelie.

Windjammer — A supercharger.

Wipe — To beat.

Zoomies — Upswept exhaust headers on dragsters. The design serves several purposes: it provides downward pressure on the rear slicks; it heats the rubber compound for maximum traction; and it blows the smoke from the spinning tires away from the driver's face.

INDEX